Praise for *Antisexist*

"If you read only one thing this year, read *Antisexist*. Beautifully written, yet mincing no words when it comes to holding the reader accountable, this book makes the business, moral, and personal case for combatting sexist attitudes and behaviors in our own lives and communities. The pages are jam-packed with poignant stories from women about the lived experience of sexism—often exacerbated by intersectional identities—and men at various stages in their own journey as accomplices and co-conspirators for change. We all own responsibility for banishing sexism, and this amazing book is where our antisexist journey begins."

—W. Brad Johnson, PhD, Professor, United States Naval Academy
and co-author of *Good Guys: How Men Can Be Better Allies for*
Women in the Workplace

"Thank you, Lynn Schmidt, for writing a perfect book for this moment. *Antisexist* provides men and women alike with a clear understanding of how sexism harms girls and women, as well as practical tips for creating a more equal world. Schmidt's book is full of maddening statistics as well as compelling, often heart-wrenching stories. "If you weren't angry about sexism before reading this book, you should be now," Schmidt writes. I *was* angry about sexism after reading the book, and I'm glad to have Schmidt's guidance on how to do something about it."

—Ed Frauenheim, Co-author of *Reinventing Masculinity:*
The Liberating Power of Compassion and Connection

"Lynn Schmidt and the essay authors hold nothing back in this accessible, blunt, truth-telling of the daily realities of women and girls. Their stories shine a jarring spotlight on sexism. For those who still say, "women are equal now," or "sexism isn't a problem anymore," please stop. Your denial is part of the problem. As Dr. Schmidt says, "denial isn't working." To every man holding this book, reading it is not enough. Real men speak up. Real men stand up. Real men are antisexist."

—jona olsson, Director with cultural bridges to justice and volunteer Fire and Emergency Medical Services Chief

"With *Antisexist*, Lynn Schmidt has delivered a much-needed new toolkit that is a concise and practical guide for anyone who wants to truly "show up" and take action as a co-conspirator and collaborator with women to stamp out sexism. Men and women ready to launch their journey toward being antisexist will find this book filled with relatable experiences and actionable strategies for translating their good intentions into meaningful action and outcomes. A must-read for any manager or leader!"

—David G. Smith, PhD, Associate Professor in the Johns Hopkins Carey Business School and co-author of *Good Guys: How Men Can Become Better Allies for Women in the Workplace*

"*Antisexist* is the book that every senior leader working to achieve gender equality in their workplace should read. It is compelling, concise, and actionable. Dr. Schmidt makes being antisexist accessible to everyone."

—Marie Hemingway, Founder and CTO, Speak Out Revolution

"Men will find *Antisexist* sobering, humbling, and challenging—analogous to the way that George Floyd's murder was in prompting soul-searching and self-reflection about white privilege. *Antisexist* will turbo-charge men as allies in the fight against sexism and gender inequity. Women will be inspired by Dr. Schmidt's passion and wisdom for her mission of transforming helplessness to hopefulness, despair into determination, and anger into action."

—**Rick Brandon, PhD, President, Brandon Partners and author of** *Straight Talk*

"Dr. Lynn Schmidt has written a thought-provoking book to address sexism. Sexist behaviors create a high cost financially and non-financially to the bottom-line of organizations and nations. These costs include turnover, poor employment brand image, lower productivity, and other impacts reflected in Schmidt's Four Outcomes of Sexism matrix. *Antisexist* will help you gain critical insights into the challenges women face due to sexism, along with practical strategies on how to address the issues. Dr. Schmidt's latest book offers sage advice to help create a world where women and girls can reach their full potential."

—**Dr. Edward E. Hubbard, Author of** *Intentional Diversity Transformation: How to Build an Inclusive Culture Using Transformational Analytics*

"It's not enough to not be sexist. We need more antisexists. Antisexists speak up and advocate for real systemic change. Dr. Schmidt lays out the action plan for all humans to be active allies against sexism."

—**Julie Kratz, Author of** *Allyship in Action* **and gender equity advocate and speaker**

"*Antisexist* is powerful and timely; an unsettling, necessary, and encouraging wake-up call for men to step into action. *Antisexist* provokes and invites men to self-reflect about their often unconscious role in perpetuating sexism that can limit their allyship efforts. Dr. Schmidt's advocacy and passion for ending sexism will inspire women and motivate men. The path to being antisexist is clear, leaving no room for excuses."

—**Ray Arata, Founder, Better Man Conference and author of**
Showing Up: How Men Can Become Effective
Allies in the Workplace

"Dr. Lynn Schmidt has done a wonderful job of weaving in real-life experiences as she provides us with a better understanding of the world of women. *Antisexist* sheds light on why many of us feel the way we do and behave in certain ways. The book goes beyond that and provides actions for men and women to take to address the four outcomes of sexism. Dr. Schmidt's book is easy to understand, and her research is a great contribution."

—**Dr. Myra K. Hubbard, Author of** *W.I.S.E. UP: Women,*
Inclusion, and Self Empowerment

Other Books by the Author

Thriving from A to Z: Best Practices to Increase
Resilience, Satisfaction, and Success

Shift Into Thrive: Six Strategies for Women
to Unlock the Power of Resiliency

Integrated Talent Management Scorecards:
Insights from World-Class Organizations on Demonstrating Value

The Leadership Scorecard

Implementing Training Scorecards

Antisexist

Challenge Sexism,
Champion Women's Rights,
and Create Equality

Lynn Schmidt, PhD

Published 2022

Printed in the United States of America

ISBN (Paperback): 9781733549615
ISBN (E-Book): 9781733549622

Library of Congress Control Number: 2022902943

Cover Design and Interior Design by Megan Katsanevakis - Hue Creative

Limits of Liability and Disclaimer of Warranty

This book is dedicated to women and men who are antisexist. Thank you for challenging sexism, championing women's rights, and creating equality. You are creating a safe and equitable world for women and girls.

Contents

Author's Note

Sexism is everywhere, bro. I don't know if it's ever not somewhere.

—BILLIE EILISH

Sexism is everywhere. As I made the final edits to this manuscript, I checked the news to see what sexism-related stories were in the headlines. In England, a woman had been beaten and raped by her well-known partner. A Canadian doctor won her discrimination lawsuit against a former employer for creating a gender-based hostile work environment. In Ireland, a man murdered a young woman out for a run. A women's sports team was suing for equal pay in the United States.

The Australian of the Year, a child sexual abuse survivor, was told she needed to smile more at events. An American congresswoman was advised she would not be taken seriously by the public because she let her hair turn grey. The United Kingdom was banning virginity repair surgery. France adopted a law to raise the number of women in top management positions. The police arrested a man in India for the so-called honor killing of his daughter. That day's sexism-related headlines were never-ending, as they are every day. Many of the stories were tragic tales of violence toward women.

Unfortunately, an overwhelming number of sexist acts against women and girls occur daily. Everywhere you turn, there are many stories in the media about women being discriminated against, harassed, abused, and murdered. The truth is, you are only hearing a small percentage of the stories. So many women aren't able to share their stories. The most vulnerable can't share their experiences of daily sexist insults, discrimination at work, harassment on the street, and abuse at home. I wrote *Antisexist* to give voice to all women by sharing common experiences. No woman or girl should feel she is alone when facing sexism.

Volumes of books and research studies exist about the different types of sexism women experience worldwide. The massive amount of material on sexism is another reason I wrote *Antisexist*. I couldn't find one place to learn about the different forms of sexism that women experience globally.

The subject matter experts and books typically specialize in one area of sexism, such as sexist language, workplace harassment, job discrimination, street harassment, intersectionality, allyship, bullying, coercive control, rape, domestic violence, and femicide. Specialization is essential to go deep on a single subject for systemic change. A broader perspective of sexism against women and the worldwide impact is needed to be antisexist.

Antisexist is focused on ending sexism toward women and girls. Women's lives are a never-ending barrage of sexist acts committed by women and men, often so frequent that it becomes normalized and accepted. I've experienced various acts of sexism, including sexist insults, biases based on nonstereotypical behavior, wage gaps as compared to my male peers, management responsibility without the title or pay, sexual harassment on the job, cyberbullying, and street harassment including flashing. Once I had my drink spiked in a bar and became violently ill. Fortunately, my friends were able to get me home safely. I don't know of one woman who couldn't provide as long a list, or longer. Women should not have to fear for their safety or fight for equality every single day.

I wrote *Antisexist* because women deserve better. *Anitsexist* doesn't ask women to lean in, lean out, or pretend to be something they aren't to have a safe and meaningful life. Women are not to be blamed for being disrespected, discriminated against, harassed, raped, or abused. We live in a patriarchal society where aspects of sexism, including harassment and violence, are problems that men need to solve. While not all men harm women, all men allow sexism to exist. Men need to understand the difference between individual fault and collective responsibility. Men are collectively responsible for their silence and lack of action that allows sexism to exist. If all men stepped up to end sexism, it would end tomorrow.

Another reason I wrote *Antisexist* is that women's rights aren't progressing. Sexism is getting worse, and there is widespread denial that it exists. The United Nations won't be able to achieve its goals by the established target dates, harassment and violence against women are growing, the percentage of women in management roles has stayed stagnant for twenty-five years, the economic costs of sexism are increasing, women's rights are slowly being eroded, and no country has established gender equality.

While the definition of feminism appears simple, the confusion and disagreement about what feminism is or isn't is not advancing women's rights. I am a feminist, and feminists have been a driving force for gender equality. I also believe that a focus on being antisexist is a more straightforward route to engaging people to stop sexism. It's simpler to say that those who aren't antisexist are sexist. For those who do not want to be associated with feminism, reading this book doesn't require declaring yourself a feminist.

Antisexist isn't about touting the positive statistics achieved in recent decades in the arena of women's rights; it's about facing reality. It's not about man-hating; it's about each of us, men and women, taking individual and collective responsibility. This book identifies how sexism impacts women and girls. For that reason, *Antisexist* does warrant a *trigger warning*. Topics covered, including street harassment, rape, domestic violence, and femicide, could trigger those who have been abused or have loved ones who have experienced violence.

Writing a nonfiction book is rarely a solitary effort. A significant source of the insights in this book came from recent original research I conducted through interviews and surveys of women worldwide to get their perspectives on sexism. I reviewed current research on sexism related to issues women encounter and the role of male allies. Because the volumes of information on sexism can be confusing, I created the Four Outcomes of Sexism matrix to make it simpler to understand the impact of sexism. Giving voice to other people's perspectives is important to me. I collected essays and anonymous short stories to share others' experiences and illustrate the core concepts. These essays and brief stories from around the world provide insight into the impact of sexism.

Another purpose of this book is to present a simple road map for readers to be antisexist. While you can't eliminate your biases, you can become aware and manage them. Then you can challenge sexism. Each chapter ends with action planning ideas, including the essays. *Antisexist* concludes with the Antisexist Action Plan. The three main goals of the book are to:

1. Enable you to understand what sexism is and its impact on women.
2. Help you to manage sexism when you experience it.
3. Assist you in becoming antisexist by challenging sexism, championing women's rights, and creating equality.

And finally, I wrote *Antisexist* because we need to end sexism. It has become normalized and accepted worldwide, producing devastating effects on women, men, children, and nations. Progress cannot be made when half the world's population is treated as less than and left behind. Choose to be antisexist, stop sexism, and create a safe and equitable world for women and girls.

ONE

Be Antisexist

The abuse of women and girls is the most pervasive and unaddressed human rights violation on earth. Women's inequality has profoundly affected our world.

—Jimmy Carter

Everyone is sexist toward women and girls to varying degrees. Research conducted by the United Nations found that almost 90 percent of people worldwide, men and women, have at least one deeply ingrained bias toward women. The study represented 75 countries, almost 80 percent of the global population. The deeply ingrained biases identified are related to politics, economics, education, violence, and reproductive rights. Many countries are backsliding in their gender-equality initiatives. No country is on track to achieve its gender-equality goals within the next ten years.

Even if you don't have a deeply ingrained bias toward women in those areas, you probably have other types of sexist biases. Sexism has become normalized in many ways. Sexism, which is prejudice, stereotyping, or discrimination based on sex or gender or the belief that men are superior to women, is harmful and disproportionately affects women and girls. It can cause feelings of worthlessness, fear, behavioral changes, and poor health. It impacts every level of society, from governments and institutions to relationships. Sexism lies at the root of gender inequality.

Sexism begins with prejudice. If you are sexist, you are prejudiced, or biased, against women and girls. Your bias is based on myths, stereotypes, and generalizations that you learn from others. A bias can be explicit, which means you are aware of it, or implicit, which means you are not consciously aware of it. Implicit and explicit biases are also referred to as unconscious or conscious biases. Our sexist tendencies can originate from many places, including our hometown, country, culture, school, family, friends, work colleagues, books, television shows, movies, and social media. Biases include beliefs about a woman's appearance, communication style, marital status, career choice, and caretaking role.

Someone sexist shows prejudice and stereotyping against women through microaggression, discrimination, harassment, or violence. Everyone commits sexist microaggressions, though many people learn to manage their biases. A person who is antisexist opposes sexism and manages their sexist biases. They take action by challenging sexism and those who are sexist.

Claiming to be non-sexist—neither sexist nor antisexist—is not an option. Saying you are non-sexist is simply an excuse to do nothing. Saying you are non-sexist indicates you believe you don't have to manage your sexism or take action to stop the sexist behaviors of others. The purpose of this book is to help you understand sexism, how to manage it when you experience it, your role in perpetuating it, and how to stop it. *Antisexist* unapologetically focuses solely on sexism toward those who self-identify as, or could be perceived as, women and girls.

The similarities and differences between feminism and sexism can confuse people, and many individuals are put off by feminism. Some don't want to be thought of as feminists. Sexism, which is prejudice, stereotyping, or discrimination toward women and girls, is a root cause of the microaggression, discrimination, harassment, and violence that women experience. Feminism is the advocacy of women's rights based on equality of the sexes. What often causes confusion is that feminism is a range of social movements and ideologies that aim to define and establish equality of the sexes. *Antisexist* is not focused on turning you into a feminist; it's focused on helping you to be antisexist.

Jennifer's Story

Jennifer left the world the same way she entered it, helpless. Never fully understanding the role that sexism played in her life and death. She was caught in a trap for most of her brief life. A trap that many women and girls stumble into, unaware and often without the tools and resources needed to escape.

When she was born, her parents welcomed her into their lives with open arms, thrilled to add a little girl to their growing family. Jennifer's two older brothers were excited to have a sister. She was sent home wrapped in a pink blanket with a wardrobe of pink onesies that said Princess, Daddy's Girl, and Little Cutie. As a young child, she played with her dolls and tea set that were gifts from her parents. When she attempted to play with her brothers' trucks, she was told those were toys for boys, not girls. She watched movies and read books about princesses saved by princes. She excelled in most subjects in school but found it hard to convey her knowledge. Her attempts to answer the teachers' questions were ignored as the boys were called on first. The teachers often complimented her for being quiet and well behaved, as girls should be.

As a teenager, Jennifer attended church each Sunday with her family. She learned that a woman's role was to support her husband. When her mother went back to work part-time, Jennifer was expected to clean the house and fix dinner for her brothers and father. She continued to excel in school and developed an interest in math and science. She talked with her school counselor about her interest in taking college preparatory courses in science. She was told that science wasn't a good career path for a girl. When she asked to join the science club, teachers told her to join a club more appropriate for girls.

At 16, she got a job waitressing in a local restaurant. One night she worked late at the restaurant. After everyone else had left, the manager asked to speak to her in the office. He asked her how things were going as he rubbed her arms and shoulders. He complimented her work. From then on, he scheduled her to work late at the restaurant at least once a week. The manager often invited her into his office when she worked late, and the rubbing and touching continued. Then one night, he pushed himself against her. He rubbed his crotch against her while telling her how beautiful she was. She didn't know what to do. She was ashamed and embarrassed. The manager threatened to tell everyone she came on to him if she didn't keep quiet. She told no one what happened and asked not to work late shifts because of her school schedule.

When Jennifer was 17, she met Matt at a friend's house. Matt was 27 and had recently moved back to town. The connection was instantaneous, and the relationship progressed quickly. Soon Jennifer was only spending time with Matt, and her other friendships slipped away. Matt told her he didn't want to share her with anyone when she suggested spending time with her girlfriends. Jennifer felt flattered. Within a matter of months, she was pregnant. Matt proposed and urged a quick wedding at the city hall. Jennifer told her parents, who had never met Matt. They were concerned and angry but agreed to the marriage. Shortly after her high school graduation, Matt and Jennifer were married. Once married, he asked her to quit her job to stay home with the baby.

After the birth of their son, Jennifer quickly became pregnant again. Jennifer took care of her children during the day and Matt at night after their daughter was born. She rarely saw her parents and had lost contact with her friends. She relied on Matt for money and had no car or credit cards of her own. Matt began stopping by the bar after work with his friends. When he got home, he was often angry at Jennifer and criticized her cooking or housekeeping. The criticism became frequent, along with yelling and swearing. Then one night, he slammed her against the wall and slapped her hard. He apologized and told her how much he loved her the following day. But the criticism, yelling, and hitting continued, along with the apologies. Often the abuse happened in front of the children.

Jennifer felt isolated and alone. One day, after a particularly violent evening with Matt, she visited her mother with the children. She hadn't seen her parents in months. Jennifer's mother was shocked when she saw Jennifer's face and a black eye. She convinced Jennifer to go to the police station to file a complaint. They left the children with Jennifer's dad and drove to the police station. The police asked Jennifer if she was sure she wanted to file a complaint against her husband. They asked her why she hadn't reported any of this abuse previously. She was asked why she hadn't gone to the hospital. While Jennifer was being questioned, her father called, telling her that Matt had come to the house to pick up the children. Jennifer didn't know where he and the children were. She was afraid he might hurt them.

Jennifer finished filing the complaint. She told the police that her husband had her children and she had to find them. She told her mother she had to go home and wait for Matt. Late that night, Matt came home with the children. He knew Jennifer had gone to the police station. He apologized once again and told her he loved her. The next day Jennifer went to the police station and redacted her statement. She said it all had been a misunderstanding, and everything was fine. Then she went home.

Matt returned home that evening after drinks at the bar. He walked into the house and shot and killed Jennifer and their two children. He then turned the gun on himself. All four were found dead the next day. Jennifer was 22 years old; her two children were three and four. Jennifer died helpless. Nothing had prepared her to understand how to escape domestic violence and coercive control by a man she loved.

Unfortunately, Jennifer's story is familiar. Women are faced with the consequences of sexism daily. One in three women worldwide experience some form of physical or sexual abuse. Globally, an average of 137 women and girls are killed daily by an intimate partner or family member. The majority of the perpetrators of these acts of violence toward women are men, and home is the most dangerous place for women. Sexism is at the core of these tragic stories. Microaggression, discrimination, harassment, and violence are all escalations that begin with sexist biases toward women.

Being antisexist includes acknowledging that while it's not all men that harm women, for women, it is all men because women don't know which men they can trust. Saying it's "all men" is not man-hating. If men are offended by anyone saying it's "all men," they need to be angry with men, the perpetrators, not women. Men that attempt to manage their sexism, who try not to be sexist, are often still part of the problem. Until men become antisexist and stand up for women against sexist and abusive men, it is "all men." Men must stop accepting sexist jokes, inappropriate comments, and demeaning behavior toward women. Men need to speak up against other men who discriminate, harass, or abuse women. Acceptance of these behaviors perpetuates sexism and behaviors that can escalate to violence.

A male university classmate and I interviewed for an engineering position in a large computer company. My classmate and I were graduating with the same degree. We knew each other well as we attended several classes together. Our credentials at graduation differed significantly, and I had the advantage. I had a higher GPA (magna cum laude), an additional two summers of intern experience with prestigious companies in my field of study, and was the recipient of my university's highest award given for leadership and non-academic contribution. The hiring manager selected my classmate for the job. The hiring manager called me to explain that while I had excellent credentials, one of his key considerations was that I would have been unhappy as a woman living in a city where women (nurses) outnumbered men because of the vast medical facility in town.

—Shelly, United States

Foundations of Sexism

Homer's *Odyssey*, which took place almost 3,000 years ago, is one of the first recorded examples of sexism and describes a man silencing a woman because her opinion was not valued. Early in the poem, when Penelope voices her judgment about a song the bard is singing, her young son Telemachus tells her to go back to her quarters and take up her women's work. He goes on to say that speech will be the business of men. Penelope goes upstairs, silenced. Women have been silenced over the centuries, and they continue to be silenced today. While progress toward ending sexism and creating equality has been made in many countries, it's been slow and hard-won. Stopping sexism and achieving gender equality is an ongoing battle. It's often one step forward, then two steps backward.

It took centuries for women to begin to get equal rights. It wasn't long ago that women not only didn't have the right to vote but also couldn't own land, travel freely, or work outside of traditional roles in many countries. In the United States, women were granted the right to vote in 1920. At that time, the right to vote benefited white women almost exclusively due to Jim Crow laws and other barriers for many women of color. Women were granted the right to vote in New Zealand in 1893 and Australia in 1902. In Saudi Arabia, women were not allowed to vote until 2011.

> *In the late 70s, I worked in an office of women. We were talking of the promise of equal pay in the future. Our male boss was outraged. He stood in the middle of the room and said, "You stupid women, if equal pay becomes law, we'll sack you all and hire men."*
>
> **—Nikki, England**

In the early 1970s women in the United States were still unable to get their own credit cards, avoid being fired for getting pregnant, take legal action against sexual harassment, and deny their husbands sex. Women worldwide continue to fight for equal rights. Any progress made toward women's rights anywhere is always at risk of being taken away when the opportunity presents itself to those in power.

Power, getting someone else to do what you want them to, is a foundation of sexism. The belief that women must be controlled and kept powerless is at its core. In most cultures, power belongs to men, not women. Gender affects power, from the highest political offices to the relationships at home. When men, women, and children are asked to close their eyes and think of a manager, CEO, judge, police chief, president, prime minister, or anyone in a culturally powerful role, the image that typically appears is male. Power equals masculinity. Inequalities between men and women shape the distribution of power. Sexism is how those inequalities are established and kept in place.

> *In my late twenties, I was thrilled to take on a new role leading international communications for our business. I was also pregnant with my first child and incredibly excited to be starting a family. I remember walking into one of our senior*

leaders' offices and talking through some new ideas about our international approach. He sighed and gave me a pitying look, and told me we'd have to figure out what to do because "You can't do that kind of job and travel if you're having a baby." I was shocked. I didn't respond at the moment. I later reported the exchange to human resources, who suggested I'd misheard him. Weeks later, he and our vice president announced that they'd divided my international job into two roles.

—Johanna, United States

One purpose of *Antisexist* is to keep the road map to being antisexist simple. To create a common language related to sexism, definitions are provided for a few frequently used terms and an explanation for how they are used in the book.

- Sexism: Prejudice, stereotyping, or discrimination, typically against women or girls, based on sex. It often includes the belief that men are superior to women. This book focuses only on sexism toward women and girls. When used in this book, the terms women and girls include anyone who self-identifies as a woman or girl or anyone who others perceive to be a woman or girl.
- Sexist: Showing prejudice, stereotyping, or discrimination against women through microaggression, discrimination, harassment, or violence.
- Antisexist: Opposing sexism while managing personal sexist biases. A person who is antisexist takes action by challenging sexism and those who are sexist.
- Misogyny: Hatred or contempt for women. It is a form of sexism used to keep women at a lower social status than men, thus maintaining the societal roles of the patriarchy.
- Misogynist: A person who dislikes, despises, or is strongly

prejudiced against women and may commit acts of microaggression, discrimination, harassment, and violence.

- Patriarchy: A system of society or government in which men hold the power and women are largely excluded from it. Patriarchy is a system that women can support, just like men can support feminism.
- Feminism: The advocacy of women's rights based on the equality of the sexes.
- Feminist: A person who supports feminism and believes in the equality of the sexes. Some individuals are uncomfortable with the feminist movement. They don't think that feminism and the feminist movement align with their values. This is not a book on how to become a feminist. This book focuses on being antisexist, opposed to and challenging sexism.
- Intersectionality: A concept used to describe how social categorizations are interconnected and create interdependent systems of discrimination and disadvantage. Examples are sexism and racism, sexism and ageism, and sexism and ableism.
- Implicit sexism: Sexist attitudes, stereotypes, or opinions that a person has that operate outside of their awareness and can directly contradict stated beliefs and values. It's dangerous as it creeps into a person's behavior and is outside of their complete understanding. It is also referred to as unconscious sexism or bias. Everyone has implicit biases, and people often don't realize their bias exists until someone points it out.
- Explicit sexism: A person is very clear about their sexist attitudes. Related behaviors and decisions are conducted with intent. It is also referred to as conscious sexism or bias. While you can't eliminate your sexist biases, implicit or explicit, you can become aware of and manage them. Creating awareness of sexism is one of the purposes of this book.

In my country, sexism is still prevalent, which is disheartening. A man with less experience and intelligence is preferred to be the leader rather than a very experienced and brilliant woman. I'm a woman with a good reputation, and my work speaks for itself, but sexism makes it difficult for me to progress in my career. I believe men and women are equal in terms of their capabilities.

—Adebola, Nigeria

There are six types of sexism that help explain the different forms of sexist prejudice: institutional, interpersonal, internalized, hostile, benevolent, and ambivalent sexism.

- Institutional Sexism: When policies, procedures, programs, attitudes, or laws reinforce sexist practices in an entire organization or system, such as a company or legal system. Examples are a lack of gender diversity in company leadership or women being paid less than men in a company or country.
- Interpersonal Sexism: Sexism manifests itself in interactions with others at work, at home with family members, or with strangers. Examples are making inappropriate comments about how a woman is dressed, sharing sexist jokes, or judging someone for not fitting into the stereotypes of femininity.
- Internalized Sexism: Refers to sexist beliefs that women or girls have about themselves. A person adopts these beliefs involuntarily due to exposure to sexist behavior. This can lead to feelings of self-doubt, powerlessness, or shame. It may cause women to be sexist unintentionally. Examples are self-deprecating jokes about being a woman, embarrassment about certain aspects of being female, or basing self-worth on men's perceptions.
- Hostile Sexism: Any explicitly hostile attitudes about women, including misogyny or the hatred of women. Hostile sexism

is dangerous and can lead to discrimination, harassment, and violence toward women and girls. Examples include sexist insults, victim blaming based on how a woman was dressed when raped, or sexual assault.

- Benevolent Sexism: Women are considered naturally kind, innocent, and nurturing. These beliefs stem from the opinion that women are weaker than men, making benevolent sexism harmful. Examples are focusing praise on a woman's appearance rather than on what she has accomplished or thinking that a woman cannot manage money because of her gender.
- Ambivalent Sexism: This is a combination of benevolent and hostile sexism and can be harmful. For example, if a person has a benevolent sexist view that mothers with young children should stay at home and then a mother gets a job working with the person, they might display hostile sexism toward the mother by making derogatory comments about her at work.

It all started with coming to work for a team that was "perceived" as high performing, inclusive, and fun. I realized very quickly that the environment was sexist, a good old boys club, and that the organization's leader had his preferred people. I was brought in and promoted with the expectation that I'd drive a couple of critical projects. After a few weeks, I started to ask for time with the leader, my boss's boss. I needed clarity on some vital issues on the project, given its importance. I could not trust that I had what I needed to do a great job by talking to my manager, a guy who was being a messenger between the leader and me. Then, in a passive-aggressive way, I was blocked and taken out of leading the project. I tried through various means to talk to the leader and was never able to. After a few months, I realized that I had made a huge mistake in

accepting this fake promotion. I believe they just wanted to make their diversity quota. After a year of trying to move to another area, it was clear that I had to quit, which I did.
—Isabel, United States

Four Outcomes of Sexism

Many people don't understand the significant impact sexism has on women and girls, or they deny that sexism exists. As previously noted, everyone is sexist to some degree. For that reason, it's essential to understand the significant impact that sexism has on women and girls to manage sexist biases and be antisexist. Some deny sexism exists. Denial can happen for a variety of reasons. Women may not want to psychologically deal with the fact that they face microaggression, discrimination, harassment, and violence every day because they are women. They don't want to wake up each morning to that reality. Women who support the patriarchy will deny sexism exists to align with men in power.

Men may deny sexism exists because denial is easier than facing the truth. Men may not want to acknowledge what the women in their lives experience daily. Denial may happen because sexist behaviors have become normalized and are no longer recognized as sexist. Denial can also occur if someone is a misogynist. That person won't admit sexism exists as they have contempt for women. Men who don't want to stand up and support women will deny sexism exists.

Denial isn't working. It's time to admit that sexism exists and stop normalizing it. It's time to become antisexist and take action to end sexism. Sexism leads to four outcomes that are detrimental to women: microaggression, discrimination, harassment, and violence. While these terms have broader definitions elsewhere related to racism and other biases, in *Antisexist,* they are defined specific to their impact on women. These four outcomes of sexism are all forms of abuse.

| FOUR OUTCOMES OF SEXISM ||
Microaggression	Discrimination
Sexist Language Stereotypes Objectification Shaming Mansplaining Invalidation	Education Employment Wage Gap Career Healthcare Sexual
Harassment	**Violence**
Verbal Physical Online Bullying Street Flashing	Physical Sexual Emotional Economic Coercive Control Femicide

Microaggression is commonplace verbal, behavioral, or environmental slights, whether intentional or unintentional, that communicate hostile, derogatory, or negative attitudes toward women. Discrimination is the unjust or prejudicial treatment of women. It occurs when women cannot enjoy their human or legal rights on an equal basis with others. Harassment is behavior that intimidates, demeans, humiliates, or embarrasses women and is disturbing, upsetting, or threatening. Violence against women is acts of violence that result in physical, sexual, or mental harm or suffering to women, including threats, coercion, or deprivation of liberty. The six topics listed within each outcome on the matrix are critical issues; not all related topics are listed.

There are many reasons to be antisexist. It's the right thing to do for more than half of the world's population. The various forms of abuse that women experience daily run from insults to femicide.

Helping women avoid the outcomes of sexism would benefit everyone. There are many research studies that show that gender equality makes organizations, countries, and the world economy more profitable and sustainable. A study from UN Women indicates that violence toward women and girls is one of the most pervasive human rights violations in the world. It happens in every country, in times of peace and war, and in public and private spaces.

Violence against women has a costly price tag. It is estimated to be 2 percent of the global gross domestic product (GDP) or 1.5 trillion dollars, approximately the size of the Canadian economy. According to the World Bank, the loss in human capital by women not having equality is as much as $160.2 trillion if it's simply assumed that women would earn as much as men. That is twice the value of the global GDP. It's time to stop sexism and all of its forms of oppression.

I used to coach basketball with my wife. She was the head coach, and I was the assistant. Early on, I learned that she had to be very careful about what she said to the male referees. Raising her voice, questioning their calls, or even asking for clarification often resulted in warnings, technical fouls, and even ejections. It rarely helped when I said anything. My yelling, cursing, questioning, and demanding explanations rarely resulted in any response. Sometimes I was rewarded by a change in their calls. We decided to switch spots to see if it was based on who was standing. It didn't matter. These male referees were not okay with a strong woman questioning them. For seven years and hundreds of games, it was the same story. Later, I did work with the referee association to change this, but it was still a big problem last I checked.

—Chris, United States

How to Use This Book

Antisexist was designed to be a practical guidebook combined with compelling stories to enable you to be antisexist. The Four Outcomes of Sexism matrix combined with specific action planning and personal stories provide a road map to becoming antisexist. The personal stories include the eleven chapter essays and several brief anonymous stories interspersed throughout the book. The essays and short anonymous stories highlight the sexist experiences of each of the authors. The three main goals of the book are to:

1. Enable you to understand what sexism is and its impact on women.
2. Help you to manage sexism when you experience it.
3. Assist you in becoming antisexist by challenging sexism, championing women's rights, and creating equality.

Chapters 3, 6, 9, and 12 explain the four outcomes of sexism and provide details on the critical issues within each of the outcomes of sexism. These four chapters end with recommended action steps you can take to challenge sexism, champion women's rights, and create equality.

Chapter 15 focuses on the intersection of sexism with other biases, including racism, ageism, and ableism. These biases, prejudices, and stereotypes are often interconnected and need to be examined together. This chapter also ends with recommended action steps you can take to challenge sexism, champion women's rights, and create equality.

Chapters 2, 4, 5, 7, 8, 10, 11, 13, 14, 16, and 17 are compelling essays that provide real-world examples of sexism based on each author's experience. The essay authors, women and men, represent various ages, professions, and geographic locations. Their powerful stories can be used to learn about the impact of sexism and how to handle it. Each of the essay authors ends their story with recommended suggestions for managing sexism.

Chapter 18 concludes the book with the Antisexist Action Plan. This chapter provides you with the opportunity to reflect on all that you learned and finalize your next steps for managing sexism and being antisexist. The book's final sections are notes, acknowledgments, and the author's biography.

While you can't get rid of your sexist biases, you can learn to manage them. *Antisexist* includes compelling examples of sexist behaviors and practical action steps that enable you to understand and manage sexism. The book provides a road map for being antisexist by challenging sexism, championing women's rights, and creating equality. Choose to stop sexism toward women and girls and create a safe and equitable world.

> *I was the chair of a nominating committee for our country club. Our final slate was two women and two men, all outstanding candidates. However, it was several women on the gender balanced nominating committee that questioned whether each of the highly competent and busy women ultimately nominated would have time to do the job. No one asked that about the men nominated.*
>
> **—Teri, United States**

Challenge Sexism, Champion Women's Rights, and Create Equality

Following is a list of actions you can take to stop sexism and be antisexist. Review the list and start creating your Antisexist Action Plan.

- Remember that "sexist" is not a four-letter word. Raise your hand and admit you are sexist.
- Reflect on your sexist beliefs about women and girls. Begin to move your biases from unconscious to conscious and create a list of your sexist biases.

- Consider where your biases came from: family, friends, media, and other places.
- Review your list and decide on one or two actions you'd like to take immediately to manage your biases and be antisexist.
- Look for examples of sexism in your day-to-day life. See what biases toward women and girls you find in daily discussions and various forms of media. Take brief notes on what you see and hear. When will you challenge sexism?
- Reread Jennifer's Story and underline or highlight all the examples of sexism you find in her story. Consider this your pre-test.

TWO
Finding My Voice
By Prerna Pickett

When I get up and work out, I'm working out just as much for my girls as I am for me, because I want them to see a mother who loves them dearly, who invests in them, but who also invests in herself. It's just as much about letting them know as young women that it is okay to put yourself a little higher on your priority list.

—MICHELLE OBAMA

Restless.

That is the word I would use to describe myself after giving birth to my oldest child. As a young mother I spent most of my days taking care of my son. Feeding him, changing his diaper, putting him down for naps, a sleep-deprived haze of overflowing baskets of unwashed laundry, a sink full of dishes, and so many other tasks falling by the wayside. It would surprise no one that by the end of each day I was tired.

Now tired made sense. Restless, on the other hand, made less sense. Hadn't I gotten everything I ever wanted? A husband, a home, and a baby I'd dreamed about for years. A stable dream that was now tangible. From the time I was in high school, whenever anyone asked me what I wanted to be when I grew up, I happily replied, "A mom."

I cringe thinking about the time I interned at my mom's office. It was the summer before my senior year. A summer I'd spent lazing around with my friends, driving the streets while listening to music too loudly, the taste of sunscreen and salty fries on our tongues, coating our hands. My mom, as the responsible party in our relationship, suggested that I intern a few days at her job as a way to bulk up my college applications. I agreed, because I was curious, but also because I hadn't really given college applications much thought, and I figured she knew what she was talking about.

I filed papers, played solitaire on the computer, tried out new restaurants in downtown Alexandria. I felt cool, sophisticated, mature. And maybe a little bit bored, because the business world wasn't what brought about my passion. One of my mother's co-workers asked if it was true that I wanted to be a mom when I grew up. I told her yes. She then asked how many children I wanted. "An even dozen!" was my reply. She laughed it off, but there was a hint of concern glinting behind the laughter.

But I refused to budge. I wanted to be a mother, so I would be a mother. And I became one. Except then things began to shift. Motherhood is so rarely the dream we make it out to be. I pictured myself baking cookies for my hypothetical children, reading them books, singing them lullabies, and sure, those things came true. But in between those soft moments of contentment was something else. Just beneath the surface. Nagging at me. Making me restless.

I wanted more. I felt guilty even thinking about it. As someone who grew up in a conservative religion, the idea of motherhood was likened to that of saintly duties. It was a calling. A gift. I bought into that sparkling image of being a mother. The one with shining counters, smiling faces, and a perfectly decorated home. No one told me what it was really like. Days spent loathing yourself with self-doubt, constant fears about your child, their safety, health, and education, and all the tears that would be shed over the guilt. So much guilt.

There began my journey. The restlessness clinging to my limbs came from some undetermined point inside my brain, and I needed to find it. Which didn't take long, if I'm being honest.

Writing had always been a pipe dream. Women like me, nobodies, didn't get published, and yet the idea persisted. For years I'd woven stories in my head, itching to get them down on paper. After the birth of my second child, the restlessness became overpowering, ringing in my ears, painting the world in uneven brushstrokes of blues and grays. I knew I couldn't ignore it any longer. Yes, it took me some time to finally dip my toes in the proverbial water that is writing, but I so rarely jumped right in when life decided to change directions on me. It always took time to get used to the new path.

That didn't erase the guilt. For so long I was told that women couldn't have it all. You either stayed at home with your children or you were a career woman; try to do both, and one or the other would suffer. But was writing at home with my children not having it all? I wasn't a power-suit-wearing kind of woman. I didn't want a career that required me to leave home from nine to five, but I wanted—no, I needed—something concrete. Something I could hold in my hands, see with my eyes. Something to overpower the little hint of bitterness slipping along my tongue.

As I started on this new journey, I quickly realized it wasn't easy. It never is. Not if it's worth it. Finding time to write while raising little ones, and having three more, made everything exponentially more difficult. It became downright impossible at times. But those few minutes I was able to carve out, I collected like grains of fine sand in the palm of my hands. The touch I so needed. Even though days and weeks would go by when I wouldn't touch my laptop or pick up a pen, I could still curl my fingers into those bits of sand and know that it was still there, waiting for me.

Meanwhile, guilt continued to erode my determination to forge on and discover my voice. That's the thing about writing; you're continually discovering your own voice. When I first started writing, I copied the styles of my favorite authors, because I didn't know what kind of writer I wanted to be. It's a lot like parenting. A game of trial and error until you finally understand what it is that works for both you and your child. There's a lot of failure, sometimes pain, but there's so much love in those moments when you catch a glimpse of your child's personality, and it clicks in your head what you have to do to help them along in their life.

For me the click with writing happened much more gradually. The stories I wanted to tell could only be told by me and no one else, but the idea of embracing my passions so fully terrified me. What did it mean if I found the joy I hadn't quite grasped in my writing instead of motherhood? Did that make me a bad mom? Would my children feel less loved? Less important?

I didn't want them to come second. But I also knew that in order to survive, I couldn't come second either. Which is another lesson I learned the hard way. I watched so many mothers around me burn out because they gave and gave and gave, without ever taking.

As time passed, I realized so much of what I was taught about motherhood was false. It is painful to take down the bricks of your former beliefs, the building crumbling bit by bit. Women are taught we can have it all, but that's not true; no one can have it all. But we can have the things that are truly important to us. It takes time and work, but it's not impossible. That was what I had to learn for myself. I didn't need to give up writing or take time away from mothering. I needed to learn that guilt was normal, that there was no remedy to fitting in all of the important things in my life.

I started off small. A half hour three times a week for me, for my writing. In that half hour I managed to cram so much in. I wrote like a speed demon, hell-bent on winning a race I ran alone. I told family and friends about my dream. I stopped making excuses. I embraced my passions. And never at any point did my love for my children waver. The sand I collected from writing soon became so much more. I molded it into a castle, a home, a place of safety, a place where I could be more myself, where I was allowed to be honest. A place that my children could visit with me. They became a part of that intricate pattern that is my writing life. I wove them in, using their magic to create new stories.

There are still struggles, even now. I'm still unlearning the idea that if I'm not a perfect mom, if I don't love every single minute, then I am somehow less worthy, or selfish. The guilt never truly goes away. But I'm less restless, more grounded. More comfortable in my own skin. I've found my voice. A voice that is willing to learn and grow, a voice that I can share with others through my writing.

So how did I get there? To the point where I felt like I was myself again? The point where my voice filtered through the cluttering noise of everyday life? It took years, lots of trial and error, and many tears. Nothing good comes without some pain, without a fight, but for those who might be in the same boat I was, here are a few thoughts and ideas that helped me to get to where I am today.

- There is no right way to be a mother. You need to find what works for you. The most important thing is that your children feel loved and safe, and that you do, too.
- Put yourself on the priority list, like Michelle Obama said. You can't take care of others if you aren't taking care of yourself. Scrape time out of the day that's just for you. Make sure your family knows and that they respect that time.
- Celebrate every little success. Whether it's your children's successes or your own.

- You don't have to be happy all the time. I think so often everyone assumes that if you don't enjoy every single moment of mother- hood, you're a failure. That's not true. It's normal to feel upset, sad, or restless, like I did. Allow yourself to feel your emotions.
- Don't be afraid to fail. It's going to happen. Don't listen to your internal voice based on sexist stereotypes about women. You can step outside of traditional boundaries. Don't allow it to hold you back.

Biography

Prerna Pickett believes in magic, fairy tales, and unicorns. Writing was always her dream job, and now she gets to live the dream. When Prerna isn't writing, she can usually be found daydreaming about writing, or at the library helping her five kids choose books. *If You Only Knew* is her debut novel and is published with Swoon Reads/Macmillan. You can find more information on her website, prernapickett.com. She is also fairly active on Twitter and Instagram. Her handles are as follows:

Twitter: @prernapickett

Instagram: @watchprernawrite

THREE

Four Outcomes of Sexism: Microaggression

It [microaggression] isn't about having your feelings hurt. It's about how being repeatedly dismissed and alienated and insulted and invalidated reinforces the differences in power and privilege.

—Dr. Roberto Montenegro

"She's bossy. She's abrasive. She's jailbait. She's too old for this job. She runs like a girl. She dresses like a slut. She's not leadership material. She asked for it. She doesn't deserve equal pay. She's a working mother. She'll get pregnant and quit. She acts like a man. She's a ball-buster. She needs to get a husband. She's a girly girl. She's hormonal. She's having a blonde moment. She let herself go. She's a female engineer. She's too emotional."

You may have said a few of these statements, or something similar based on your language or culture, about a woman. You are like most everyone else in the world if you have uttered a sexist statement about a woman. In fact, you've probably made more than one sexist comment about women. Now is the time to raise your hand and admit it. Sexist language, stereotypes, objectification, and shaming are harmful and can cause discrimination, harassment, and violence toward women. Girls begin to feel the impact of sexist comments as soon as they understand language. These comments can impact a child's self-esteem, causing them to feel anxious and unsafe and may lead them to withdraw from social and educational interactions.

The first of the four outcomes of sexism is microaggression. Microaggression is commonplace verbal, behavioral, or environmental slights, whether intentional or unintentional, that communicate hostile, derogatory, or negative attitudes toward marginalized groups, specifically women and girls for this book. Environmental slights are subtle acts of discrimination that occur within society. An example is a college campus that only has buildings named after white men.

The use of sexist microaggressions has become normalized in the media. It is how many men and women express their sexism, often unconsciously. It can be so subtle that you might not even notice. Sometimes a sexist comment is delivered in the form of a supposed compliment. A man may tell a woman that she does something well for a woman. Women and those witnessing incidents involving microaggression are often left wondering what happened. Some sexist microaggressions have become so normalized that women will make demeaning comments about themselves. A woman may call herself ditzy or say she is having a blonde moment.

While microaggressions may appear small, they aren't. They are a form of abuse. Years of being stereotyped, shamed, and objectified can make women feel unsafe. It can cause feelings of inferiority, distress, anxiety, and depression. Those who speak up about microaggressions might be labeled as overly sensitive or too politically correct. Criticizing sexist behaviors can lead to women and their allies being ridiculed and silenced. People in power may use their positions to manipulate those experiencing microaggression into believing they are wrong. Microaggression perpetuates the patriarchy while silencing women.

In a study of women in corporate America, 64 percent reported experiencing microaggressions at work. Black women indicated they deal with a greater variety of microaggressions in the workplace due to the intersection of sexism and racism. Lesbians, 71 percent, said they experienced microaggressions in the form of demeaning comments, which made them unable to talk about their personal lives at work. Women who experience microaggression on the job are three times more likely to think about leaving the job than women who don't. In the United Kingdom, 66 percent of 16-to-18-year-old girls surveyed said they experienced or witnessed sexist language at school. In Europe, 80 percent of women surveyed stated they had been confronted with mansplaining or manterrupting at work.

| FOUR OUTCOMES OF SEXISM ||
Microaggression	Discrimination
Sexist Language	Education
Stereotypes	Employment
Objectification	Wage Gap
Shaming	Career
Mansplaining	Healthcare
Invalidation	Sexual
Harassment	Violence
Verbal	Physical
Physical	Sexual
Online	Emotional
Bullying	Economic
Street	Coercive Control
Flashing	Femicide

Six Types of Microaggression

Six common types of microaggression are sexist language, stereotypes, objectification, shaming, mansplaining, and invalidation. Hundreds of these slights are accepted in every culture. Each country has a long list. Sexist language has become normalized, and you may not even recognize you said or heard something sexist. Stereotypes about women are often turned into jokes or used to reward and penalize women for certain behaviors. Women are frequently objectified based on their looks and sexuality. Shaming is negative comments that insult women for what they do or how they look. Mansplainers remind women that their expertise is considered less valuable than men's, even when they know more than men. Invalidation occurs when women's experiences related to sexism are dismissed.

> *At one of the companies I worked at, there was a man considered extremely smart and talented. However, he had a drinking problem and would disappear for two hours. He would come back drunk and corner me in the kitchen, letting me know I had no purpose in the company. This behavior was repeated multiple times. The other employees were told to leave the office if this individual came to the office drunk. In most cases, the two owners had left for the day. After several incidents, I confronted one of the owners about this individual's behavior. I was told the problem was not him but me because I had tits.*
> **—Jessica, Canada**

Sexist Language

Sexist language is microaggression that makes women invisible and is patronizing. When people talk about "mankind," they express an implicit belief that men are the most important part of humankind. When the pronoun "he" is used about someone of unknown gender in a stereotypically male profession, women in that profession are discounted.

Patronizing words minimize women's achievements and have no masculine equivalent word. Examples are career woman, working mother, housewife, soccer mom, mompreneur, and female engineer (or any profession). Other patronizing words are sweetheart, sweetie, and girly girl. It's patronizing women to say, "That's good for a woman (or girl)."

> *When I was eight months pregnant, I attended a meeting on-site with a client team in another province. The male partner at the meeting had just bought a toolbox and toolset for his wife's birthday. He asked me to transport it back to our home office for him on the return flight, as he had overpacked and didn't want cargo surcharges. I was already carrying my laptop bag, overnight bag, purse, and materials for the client presentation. I said to him, "You're asking your pregnant colleague to transport your wife's heavy gift?" He tried to justify the request, and I explained why it was inappropriate.*
> —**Marcela, Canada**

Stereotypes

Stereotypes about women can be microaggressions that have become commonplace and are often considered funny topics of conversation. Jokes are made about how women nag their partners and aren't good drivers. They are all supposedly in good fun while it perpetuates beliefs that women are inferior. Sexist stereotypes that create double standards tend to punish women for certain behaviors that are acceptable for men.

One stereotype is that women are polite, nurturing, caring, warm, and helpful. When women demonstrate stereotypically masculine qualities like assertiveness and confidence, they are often labeled as pushy, bossy, aggressive, abrasive, or bitchy. Women are damned if they do and damned if they don't. If women behave as stereotypically feminine, they are discounted because they are perceived as weak females. If they act stereotypically masculine, they are discounted because they are perceived to be bitches.

Expecting a woman to take notes at a meeting and get the coffee, or mistaking a woman for a nurse when she is the doctor are other examples of stereotypes. Sexist words for women that reflect stereotypes are drama queen, nag, catty, bitchy, diva, ladylike, bubbly, and flirty. Blonde jokes and references to a woman being a "Karen" in the United States are also demeaning. A general rule is if you wouldn't say it about a man, don't say it about a woman. There is no equivalent to a blonde joke or the Karen label for men. Those words exist to make women feel inferior. Women with internalized sexism may use stereotypical microaggressions in their verbal and written communications. They may use words like just, actually, sorry, and other terms that undermine their communications.

> *When I directed the advertising and marketing of a large automotive company, many men asked me how I, a woman, could run a car brand. It seemed strange to them that a woman was qualified enough to talk about engines and horsepower. Later, I worked in the oil industry, surrounded by male engineers who didn't want me to speak or give opinions in work meetings. I believed it was my right to speak and give my opinion if I did not agree with something. Or so I thought, until one day they told me, "You are here to continue processes; forget about the rest." That was when I began to coldly analyze if the company was the right place for me. In our Latino countries, there is a lot of discrimination in the workplace. Men believe that women shouldn't have equal pay or work in men's jobs. It is a huge challenge for Latino women to work to change this.*
>
> **—Adriana, Mexico**

Objectification

Objectification is used as a microaggression when women are demeaned based on their appearance or sexuality. Women are taught that their worth lies in their looks, and if they don't have the body, face, or attire considered attractive in their culture, they have no value. The inference is that being sexually appealing to men is a priority. On the other hand, women are advised not to wear revealing clothing and dress more modestly, insinuating that how women dress reflects their morals.

Words used to refer to women who aren't perceived as dressing appropriately are slut, frigid, tease, prude, jailbait, and hussy. Women are taught that how they dress makes them vulnerable to harassment or assault. Women are victim blamed when they are sexually assaulted or harassed. They are accused of wearing too little or drinking too much, when the truth is that no matter what the victim was doing, the rapist is responsible for raping her.

The media and peers pressure women to try the latest fad diet or exercise more so that men don't lose interest. This can lead to eating disorders. Women who are overweight are harassed and often referred to as fat, curvy, and plus-size. As women age, many societies no longer consider them sexually attractive and refer to them as faded beauties or frumpy. Older women that are considered attractive are demeaned by being called cougars. A woman who isn't stereotypically feminine may be referred to as a man-hater, tomboy, ball-buster, dyke, or butch. Objectification is a significant issue with teenage girls. The media, including social media, is a primary culprit in contributing to teenage girls' poor body image and feelings of low self-esteem.

When I started my career in consulting, I was young, focused, and upwardly mobile. I led significant projects, overcoming logistically challenging circumstances with problem-solving and directness. A boss called me in for a review and said, "There have been some complaints about your assertiveness as a manager. You've become tell assertive, like a male." A female director in a subsequent job called me in for an informal coaching session and said, "It's your ambition that concerns me."
—**Alice, United States**

Shaming

Shaming is a microaggression that covers a multitude of imaginary sins committed by women. Women are shamed for their hormones and the process they deal with every month, menstruation. The perception of a transition from childhood to womanhood causes fear and shame. Menstruation has become the source of jokes that leads one to believe menstruation shouldn't be talked about because it's gross and painful. Unfortunately, not talking about it can cause serious health problems to go undetected. Women experiencing menopause are shamed for hormonal changes and hot flashes. Women are made to feel like menopause is an embarrassment they shouldn't discuss. It has become another excuse to joke about women's emotions rather than treating menopause as a significant healthcare issue for women. Women are described as irrational, emotional, hysterical, hormonal, and moody because of their monthly cycle or lack thereof.

Mothers are shamed for any decision they might make, including working or not working and breastfeeding or not breastfeeding. Women who breastfeed in public are shamed because they might briefly expose a breast. Mothers who bring fast food home are shamed for being lazy, whereas fathers who bring fast food home are considered fun. If women choose to remain single, they are shamed and called spinsters. They are questioned about their biological clocks, as if not having a child makes a woman incomplete. Women are once again in a lose-lose situation, whether they have children or not. It doesn't matter what the decision is; it will be the wrong one and another excuse for shaming.

> *I was labeled an aggressive female at one of the most pres-*
> *tigious multinational corporations globally, a company that*
> *prides itself on its diversity, inclusion, and equity practices.*
> *I was once told that when our two senior managers were*
> *speaking, both white males, I needed to uncross my arms,*

smile more, and nod. They said I was coming off as too serious, direct, and brusque. My body language was not a critique of what they had to say. It was simply how I look when listening closely and processing information. I furrow my brow and take things seriously. It was extremely upsetting, and I openly rejected the feedback and soon left the company. Sometimes I think companies that are the most public about equality and inclusion tend to have the most inequality and exclusive practices. They get away with it because of the stories they tell themselves, their employees, and the public. It's like being gaslit.

—Whitney, United States

Mansplaining

Mansplaining is a microaggression caused by a man condescending to a woman by explaining something to her that she already knows. This often happens when women have expertise on a topic. Mansplaining can occur in person or virtually and one-on-one or in groups. It frequently happens on social media. Mansplainers let women know that their knowledge and expertise are not as valuable as men's, even when the women know more than the men.

Another similar phenomenon is manterrupting. Both men and women interrupt women more than men. Still, men are nearly three times more likely to interrupt a woman than another man. Men interrupting women is considered a universal phenomenon that cuts across borders. Often a man will repeat the same idea as the woman he interrupted and receive credit for the idea. Women will frequently present a concept that is ignored. Later, when a man presents the same idea, everyone gets excited.

Men, and sometimes women, attempt to take control of conversations about women's issues by saying, "What about men? Men have similar issues." When this happens, the discussion becomes centered on men's issues. "But men too" dialogue is a microaggression as it attempts to take over a conversation centered on women and make it about men. Men need to create separate conversations for discussions about men.

> *I was invited to a leadership conference to give a presentation. The day before my presentation, I talked with a man at lunch. He asked me what I thought was the most critical aspect of leadership coaching. I responded, but he interrupted to mansplain to me about the coaching process before I could finish. When I started to explain what I believed was the best process, he interrupted me again to say that I should read Dr. Johnson's book on leadership coaching. He then proceeded to mansplain his interpretation of Dr. Johnson's coaching process to me. I waited for him to pause to take a breath. When he finally did, I said, "Let me introduce myself. I'm Dr. Johnson. I wrote the book you are referring to, and I'll be presenting on the topic tomorrow." He looked surprised for a brief second and then continued to tell me about my work.*
>
> —Jessica, England

Invalidation

Invalidation is a microaggression that involves dismissing women's thoughts, feelings, and experiences. When women attempt to call out the microaggressions they have experienced, they get told they are too easily offended or overly emotional. People will say things like "Just let it go," "You are overreacting," or "It's not a big deal."

Invalidation leads to the silencing of women. It causes women to silently accept injustice rather than speak up about it. The result is that the cumulative effect of microaggressions builds up and becomes problematic and detrimental to women's health and well-being. To bring an end to microaggression, women should speak up about their experiences, and men and women who have been sexist need to learn to listen and reflect on how to improve their behaviors.

Microaggression tends to be how men and women express their sexism toward women, and unfortunately, it often isn't addressed. Committing a sexist microaggression doesn't necessarily mean you are a terrible person; it means that you live in a patriarchal society where sexism has become normalized. Be aware that microaggression causes harm. Microaggressions are difficult for everyone who experiences them. They also become the building blocks for other outcomes of sexism, including discrimination, harassment, and violence. A sexist society does not allow all of its members to thrive. It's time to be antisexist and stop sexist microaggression.

> *I have always used the last name I was born with, my father's last name, even after I got married. After my wedding, people would tell me I had to change my last name to my husband's name. This has never been mandatory legally in my country. The tradition was, and is, so deeply rooted that until recently, people were convinced it was mandatory for a woman, once married, to give up her name and be referred to, or reduced to, her husband's wife. Later I realized that when filling out forms and indicating both my last name and maiden name, I would "disappear" and be registered only under my spouse's name. This regularly leads to confusion when dealing with official administrations and banks as I do not exist under my last name in their computer files.*
>
> **—Lucile, France**

Challenge Sexism, Champion Women's Rights, and Create Equality

Following is a list of actions that men and women can take to stop microaggression and be antisexist. Review the list and add items to your Antisexist Action Plan.

- Create a list of the most frequently used microaggressions in your country, culture, and society. List the verbal, behavioral, and environmental microaggressions you encounter most often.
- Explore your own sexist biases. Observe and question your assumptions. Reflect on the six types of microaggression and list the words you say, unintentionally or intentionally, that are microaggressions. Commit to no longer using those words. Replace them with gender-neutral words if necessary.
- List your behaviors that are microaggressions and any environmental microaggressions where you want to effect change. Create a plan to change behaviors and environmental microaggressions.
- Educate your children early about sexism and microaggression so they can identify it and speak up about it. Ensure they can talk to you about it without being invalidated. Role-playing can be helpful.
- Be selective about what your children watch on television and online or read. The media is full of sexism of all types, and microaggression can be found anywhere.
- Women, men, and children can effectively deal with microaggression by redirecting it. Redirect the issue back to the microaggressor by simply asking, "What did you mean by that?" Then allow them to answer, however long that takes.
- As a woman, be more vocal about microaggression. When you experience it, speak up. Ask, "What did you mean by that?" State how it offended or upset you.
- If you are a bystander, man or woman, and witness microaggression, be an ally. As an ally, sometimes your voice can be heard more powerfully than those directly affected by microaggression. Be vocal about microaggression and speak up when you see or hear it.
- As a bystander, speak for yourself, not on behalf of the person who has experienced the microaggression, as that can be

unintentionally demeaning. Instead of saying, "You hurt her feelings," say, "Here's why I'm offended or upset."

- If you are the microaggressor and someone accuses you of a microaggression, try not to be defensive. Be open to learning more about your sexist biases. Acknowledge the other person's hurt, apologize, and reflect on where the microaggression came from and how you can avoid similar mistakes in the future.

FOUR

Fighting Stereotypes
By Fatma Noureldin

Always be ready to fight anytime, anywhere.

— ANONYMOUS

It is a fact that no matter what environment you are in, your work will speak louder when it is wrapped in the right visual communications. While I was in Egypt, I had the chance to work with many nationalities, including Europeans, Americans, and Asians, who gave me the impression that my results were all that mattered.

When I moved to Italy several years ago, I came with my old impression that Europeans deal with people based on results, while your appearance is negligible. It took me four years of interacting with many social levels of Italian society, both formally and informally, to realize that I had to resume fighting stereotypes again. This time the stereotypes were based on appearance and ethnicity.

Learning how to deal with stereotypes was an important factor in building my personality. I was born the eldest of two daughters to a middle-class Egyptian family, in a small city near Cairo, the capital.

I was fortunate because my parents raised us with more freedoms at a time when males had more freedom than females. My family didn't give us any idea that we were less free or weaker because we were females. In my city, in some families with a daughter and a son, the son would drive the car and travel abroad alone while the girl was not allowed to. If the girl was very clever and could receive an education in Cairo, she wouldn't be allowed to travel. She would have to accept a totally different type of specialization, as it depended on what education was available in her city.

Growing up and watching this in my neighborhood and in the lives of my school friends, I became more appreciative of every action my family took. My parents sent us to the best schools available in our city. My mother motivated me to take summer classes in English and not to be satisfied with the school classes. My fluency in English made me eligible to join a unique school in Cairo, which meant that I had to live away from my family. They also pushed me to get my driver's license before finishing school. Their support and empowerment were always with me, even after I finished university, worked, and started to earn my MBA.

Without this support, I believe I wouldn't have made bold decisions in my life, decisions that moved me on to achieve bigger dreams. But with each step I took, I discovered that I was encountering more stereotypes about the girls in my community. I remember when I decided to work while I was still in university, I received a negative, discouraging comment from a mother of my friend. In my city there was the perception that if a girl works while she is studying, it means that her family can't support her education and they are in need of money. Certainly, the word "self-actualization" wasn't in their dictionary yet. At that time my only objective was to get work experience and build my résumé quicker than my peers.

While I was on my journey to achieve my career goals, I had many marriage proposals. Unfortunately, most of the men were after me to complete their social image. They were not interested in me achieving my objectives, and they would stop my growth after marriage.

I reached my first big career goal and became the marketing manager of a multinational company. While preparing for the second phase of my career—having my own business—I met my husband-to-be on my second trip to Italy as a tourist. I found in him real support and understanding, which I appreciated especially after my mother, my greatest supporter, passed away. With marriage I moved into a different stage of my life. I left my beloved Egypt, family, and friends, and had to rethink my career.

The first couple of years I was in Italy, my network consisted only of expatriates. I didn't have Italian friends or acquaintances, except my husband's family. It stayed this way for about two years, until I realized that my Italian needed to be improved. It wasn't easy to talk to Italians in public offices or to medical doctors. It wasn't a nice feeling when I talked in a different accent or made a mistake in pronouncing a word.

Some Italians would be patient and try to understand what I wanted to say, others would try to hide their annoyance, and others would show it. This was not easy to accept, because in my country if a foreigner tried to speak Arabic and had an accent, we would encourage the person to say more and learn. I started to look for other ways to improve my Italian.

Being a marketer, I found opportunities to apply my craft all around me. The place where we live, a nice small community, is surrounded by the beauty of nature. I contacted the president of a local committee and gave him a list of small projects that would promote the place and provide a good income to be used in more developments. He was patient enough to listen to me, with my slow Italian and mistakes in pronunciation. At the end of our meeting he asked me to attend the upcoming meeting of the committee and share these plans. I was able to make a small presentation for the first time in Italian for Italians, and I found great acceptance and readiness to implement the ideas.

I extended my work with this committee and volunteered to teach English for free. Then when summer arrived, I participated in preparing for the yearly summer feast. This was a great opportunity to get to know more people and to improve my language skills. With time, I was able to hold deeper discussions with more Italians. This was very interesting to me, as I was able to discover things that I hadn't seen earlier. I was asked questions about my country, my religion, and my life in Egypt. The topics were based upon a stereotype of a Muslim female from the Middle East.

I learned that many were thinking similar ideas as they shared their thoughts or assumptions. Some of the stereotypes they had were:

- As I am Muslim, they believed I wore a veil when I lived in Egypt. Once I moved to Italy, they thought I took the veil off as a way of being more liberal.
- I left my country to escape because Italy is more liberal for women and has better opportunities.
- I drove only when I came to Italy, and I didn't ever drive in my country.
- I didn't have a chance to get a good education in Egypt.
- In Egypt women can't work.

Learning about their stereotypes impacted me in two ways. First, I was happy to talk with them and help them learn that things are very different from what they assumed. I am Muslim, and while living in a Muslim country I am not veiled, while my sister is veiled. Each of us had our own freedom to do what we wanted to do. I didn't escape to Italy. I came as a tourist three times. I was living in my country and had the freedom to come and go as I wanted. I owned a car when I was in Egypt and my driving license is twenty years old. I had to go to driving school in Italy, as the law doesn't allow my license to be converted. I am a university graduate with a master's degree. I learned

English, Italian, French, and German when I was in my country. I was working until the week before I moved to Italy.

Second, once I learned about their stereotypes, I felt pain for a while, as I now understood my previous interactions with some Italians. They were simply dealing with me based upon the negative stereotype of a Muslim female from the Middle East that is shown in the media. It affected work interviews, social gatherings, and many other situations in daily life. For example, dealing with the shop assistant in a clothing shop.

In some situations, I wasn't getting the proper respect Italians and others would receive. I was treated as if I was inferior. I would be followed by shopkeepers who appeared to think I might steal something. They were not welcoming or friendly.

This new awareness about the stereotypes they held made me reevaluate how I dealt with others. I had the perception that in Europe it would be easier to prove myself and my results would speak for themselves. Unfortunately, I discovered that I had to work harder in two directions. I had to do the job while addressing the stereotypes.

Changing the stereotypes they have about me continues to be difficult. I have to think carefully about every action I take, including the way I look and the way I dress. I want to shorten the time it takes to show who I am. One of the actions I took to shorten the time to introduce myself is that I reactivated my Facebook account after six years. This helps my Italian circle of acquaintances to have a chance to see who I was before coming to Italy. In my conversations I make sure to highlight how things were and are in Egypt.

I am not yet feeling that I can be myself, but things are getting better. I'm showing my self-confidence and highlighting my strengths. Most of the time I am receiving the respect I deserve. Based on my experiences, here are some suggestions to help overcome stereotyping.

- Find a supportive circle to guide you in the hard times. A family member, a friend, or a mentor. Sometimes when we feel stressed, we may tend to surrender and not resume our path to achieve our goals. A supportive person will guide you and help you clarify your perspective.
- Build your self-confidence by writing a journal of your achievements and strengths. Go through them daily. This reminder will be within you and come out when needed.
- People will judge you based upon your appearance. Learn how to use it to be aligned with your message in life and your audience.
- Be a giver, especially in new environments, as it will help you connect with others. It will be an icebreaker, and you will increase your network. It will be a good opportunity to share your expertise and display your assets.
- Explore having open discussions with people about their stereotypes to help them learn about who you really are, including information about your background and ethnicity.

Biography

Fatma Noureldin is the founder of M-Kemet in Egypt, a company that promotes the excellence of Egyptian products. With more than twenty years of experience in the marketing sector, in multinationals and local companies covering varied industries, she provides consultancy services for start-ups and young professionals. She loves reading, learning, and sharing what she learns. Her website is www.menmesr.com.

FIVE

Three Suggestions and a Confession
By Steven Howard

You may believe that you are responsible for what you do, but not for
what you think. The truth is that you are responsible for what you think,
because it is only at this level that you can exercise choice.
What you do comes from what you think.

—MARIANNE WILLIAMSON

L et's start with the confession first. I had one of the all-time worst
managerial reactions to news from a female direct report. It happened in late January, 1986. Returning from her end-of-year holiday,
my sales executive cheerily informed me that she was pregnant and
due in August. My immediate reaction? Unbelievably it was "Shit."

Thoughts of her getting two months of maternity leave flooded
my brain, followed by the fear of not meeting our sales quota for the
year. Even the look of horror and displeasure in her face to my blurted
expletive did not make me pause to celebrate this important news
with her. Rather, I started to calculate how much of my personal sales
bonus was going out the window.

None of my male bosses had taught me that this was inexcusable behavior. In fact, my own boss had the exact same reaction when I informed him that my sales lady was pregnant.

Fortunately, my colleague made me fully aware that I needed to change my thinking. Immediately. Even more fortunately, I readily did so. And, as the quote from Marianne Williamson above reflects, changing my thinking enabled my corporate career and entrepreneurial success. In fact, throughout the past two-and-a-half decades, women have been my major clients and my biggest supporters.

I grew up in the Virginia Slims era, the cigarette brand aimed at women with the slogan "You've come a long way, baby." While this cigarette brand may have intended this slogan as a laudatory message to women, many males at the time considered the tagline to also mean "You've come far enough, baby, and do not expect to go any further." In other words, be happy with your position in life and do not expect, or attempt, to go any further. This, of course, did not apply to my go-getter sales lady, who remarkably remains one of my closest and long-lasting friends. To say that we have been through a lot together over the decades since my supervisory blunder would be an understatement.

I was also raised to believe that boys like me who showed initiative or organizational skills on the playground or in school were exhibiting leadership skills. The girls in my school who attempted to do the same were usually shut down and told to stop being bossy. Unfortunately, this belittlement of young girls continues today. I wish parents, educators, and all other adults would learn to eliminate the phrase "don't be bossy" from their vocabularies when dealing with preteen girls. It may take a generation for this to become effective, but it would certainly increase the competency and confidence in displaying and demonstrating leadership skills in the women of the future.

Over the years I have learned that it is not the sole responsibility of women to teach men how to behave and act properly in the workplace.

It is also the responsibility of men to teach one another. With this in mind, here are three suggestions for men on interacting with their female colleagues in the workplace, based on my observations and the questions I often get asked as a leadership coach.

Suggestion number one is to beware of personal biases. All of us have biases. A bias is an assumption about a category of people, objects, and events that produces a prejudice in favor of or against a thing, person, or group. Biases may have positive or negative consequences. While a conscious bias is explicit, an unconscious bias is implicit. Both can impact decision-making, as well as our relationships and interactions with others, either consciously or subconsciously. Biases are not limited to ethnicity, gender, sexual orientation, or nationality. How prevalent are biases? They are more common than you may think. In my book *Better Decisions, Better Thinking, Better Outcomes* I share twenty-four biases that are fairly common.

Here's a scenario I often use in my training programs. You are the manager of an eight-member team based in the U.S. One of these team members has been on maternity leave for eight weeks and is due to return to work next week. You need one team member to go to Malaysia for three weeks, beginning three weeks from now. This female team member is one of two equally qualified employees on your team capable of handling this three-week assignment. The other is a male team member. Who will you offer the assignment to?

Well over 90 percent of the male participants in my leadership programs automatically give the assignment to the man. Most rationalize this choice, thinking, "It is obvious the female employee would not want to be separated from her newborn so soon after birth." This is the wrong answer and the wrong rationalization. The correct answer is to meet with each employee separately to assess their willingness, capacity, and personal availability for the overseas assignment. And, should either staff member decline the opportunity for personal reasons, their decision should never be held against them.

It is wrong to make assumptions about how the female team member in this situation, based on a true incident in one of my client organizations, will evaluate and desire this overseas assignment. Her spouse or other family members might be available to look after the newborn while she is away. She may consider the assignment to be an important addition to her career credentials. She and her spouse may consider going together to Malaysia with the newborn. A whole host of factors can come into play. The important learning point is that she must be given the option to evaluate this opportunity and to decide for herself if this is something that she desires and is willing to do. And male bosses should not think otherwise.

The #MeToo movement entered the business world in 2017. It encouraged and enabled thousands of women to speak up about workplace harassment. As a result, most corporations and organizations have started to take the issue of gender-related and sexual-innuendo types of harassment, misconduct, and provocations seriously, with hundreds of men losing their jobs as a result.

Unfortunately, there has been one unintended side effect from the #MeToo movement and publicity. Many male executives and managers are intentionally minimizing their contact with and their mentoring of female employees. Two surveys from 2018 of nearly 9,000 adults employed in the U.S. reported that almost half of male managers were uncomfortable in engaging in one-on-one work activities or work-related socializing with women. Even worse, these surveys showed that 16 percent of male managers were not comfortable in mentoring a female colleague. This is tragic. And unacceptable.

However, as Laura Liswood, secretary general of the Council of Women World Leaders states in a *New York Times* article (January 2019), "Basically, #MeToo has become a risk-management issue for men." But it really should not be a risk-management issue for men. Men simply need to stop crossing professional boundaries with their suggestive comments, intimations, and inferences when dealing with their colleagues. If men would stay well inside proper boundaries, they would have no legitimate reason for concern. After all, it is extremely rare for a false accusation of sexual harassment to be made. What are those boundaries not to be crossed? It's not rocket science, as this list shows.

- Refrain from making off-color jokes. If you wouldn't tell the joke to your grandmother, you probably shouldn't be telling it to your female colleague.
- Maintain physical distance. This has nothing to do with the social distancing protocols of COVID-19. Keep two to three feet, or more, of personal space between you and a colleague.
- Avoid hugging, unless it is initiated by the other person. Petting, patting, and poking a colleague is unacceptable behavior.
- Watch your facial expressions. Winking, raising eyebrows, or licking your lips can be misinterpreted as a come-on. A sincere smile is best.
- Your relationship issues are not hers to fix or sympathize with. Find a female friend outside the workplace if you want a feminine perspective or advice.
- Compliment her on her work, not her perfume, clothes, hair, or anything else personal.

There's another scenario that I am often asked about by males under thirty who are new to the role of team leader or supervisor. They want to know how to handle mentoring their female colleagues, especially when traveling together for work. The typical scenario described to me is this. When they traveled with their male bosses, they often received great mentoring and coaching in the evening hours, after client calls and business meetings. These one-on-one sessions often took place in a sports bar or similar environment where adult beverages were consumed.

However, these young men are not comfortable traveling today with their female colleagues, a sad fallout from the #MeToo movement that has produced some significant benefits to society. They prefer not to dine with their women staff members or to interact with them in any manner after the formal business meetings of the day have been completed. In fact, many of these men tell me that they even go so far as to not stay in the same hotel as their female colleagues, for fear of being falsely accused of improper behavior.

Remarkably, these men also readily admit that they know they are doing a disservice to their female employees by not spending the time mentoring them that they themselves had received. Unfortunately, their fears of a false accusation, and their similar fears of being totally defenseless against such an accusation of sexual harassment, override their desires to be good leaders. Thus, they act according to their thinking.

Here's the advice I give them for mentoring or socializing with female colleagues when traveling:

- First, always refer to the corporate policies, procedures, and guidelines of the organization in which they work.
- Remember that a key priority of all leaders is to develop their employees to their highest capabilities possible. This priority must overcome their fears.
- Choose Starbucks or a family-style restaurant over a sports bar or any other venue where alcoholic beverages are served.
- Never ask for a female colleague's room number—or give yours out.
- If staying in the same hotel, take separate elevators to your rooms. Make a phone call from the lobby if necessary, to delay going to your room while she goes to hers.
- Use Uber or Lyft over a taxi.

- Include colleagues, clients, and business partners to dinners when feasible.

Suggestion number two is to ask before helping. Many men were taught to open car doors for women, help women put their coats or jackets on, and allow women to enter first in revolving doors of an office building or hotel. As a result, many of us are confused as to when to use, or appropriately demonstrate, the societal manners we were taught in our youth. I have learned that the best policy is to ask first, with phrases such as, "May I get that car door for you?" or "May I help you with that jacket?" By politely asking first, we help both ourselves and our female colleagues navigate what can be a somewhat sticky social interaction in the workplace.

Additionally, professional women are capable and competent in finding solutions to the issues, challenges, and opportunities they are facing. They are not in need of unsolicited advice, particularly from male colleagues who start their advice with phrases like, "This is what you should do" or something similar.

Like the overseas assignment example above, it is a mistake to assume that a woman—or anyone else, for that matter—needs help, particularly in a business situation or environment. It is wrong to assume that we always know best or that a female associate or friend wants us to proffer advice on how to fix the problems they are facing. In fact, what they often desire is for us to simply listen, empathize, and ask a few good questions that help them draw their own conclusions and solutions. Similar to what an executive coach would do.

Suggestion number three is to walk the talk. As an example of how far I have personally come in recognizing the need to be more supportive of women in business, I have recently been creating draft strategies and creative concepts for the WEConnect International chapter in Mexico. WEConnect International has a mission to connect women business owners to corporate members that collectively represent over US$700 billion in annual purchasing power. The goal is for these corporations to increase their purchases from women-owned businesses around the world. It is a mission I totally support.

Recently I coached two women entrepreneurs on a pro bono basis in the development of their credentials presentation for a digital marketing opportunity with a major multinational company that is one of the WEConnect global corporate partners. They were hesitant to pursue this digital marketing opportunity because they did not have 100 percent of the requirements. I convinced them to go after it anyway, which they did.

So, like the cigarette slogan, I have come a long way in recognizing the need for myself and other males to support the continued growth of women professionals and entrepreneurs. While there is still a long way to go, for both genders, the future is certainly brighter than the caveman era in which I grew up. I am glad to see such progress. I look forward to witnessing, and contributing to, future progress for women across the world. There is no doubt in my mind that the next generations of women will have an increasingly important and leading role in this world. In summary, here are five tips to being a better male colleague, peer, co-worker, and supporter of women's advancement in the workplace.

- Become more aware of situations where your female colleagues are being ignored, overlooked, or disregarded. Be sensitive to the fact that even if you do not personally witness these actions, they are in fact occurring regularly in the life of many female workers, at all levels of almost all organizations.
- Step up and speak out any time you see a female employee being overtly or subtly harassed, demeaned, hassled, disgraced, or treated without respect.
- Show respect by staying within proper interaction boundaries at all times with all colleagues.

- If you are a manager or executive, remember that your top priority is to develop the talent of ALL your employees. Identify the ways and methods you can do so with your female staff, so that both you and they are comfortable with the environment for such coaching, mentoring, and development conversations.
- Ask before helping or giving advice. Be supportive of the decisions that they make.

Biography
Steven Howard is an award-winning author of twenty-one leadership, marketing, management, and professional development books. Steven creates and delivers virtual and classroom leadership development programs and provides 1:1 coaching for leaders at all levels of organizations. He is well known and recognized for his truly international and multicultural perspective, having lived in Singapore for twenty-one years and in Australia for twelve years. He currently resides in Southern California.

SIX

Four Outcomes of Sexism: Discrimination

*Asking you to give me equal rights implies that they are yours to give.
Instead, I must demand that you stop trying to deny me
the rights all people deserve.*

—Elizabeth Peratrovich

It will take 135 years for women to achieve parity with men on four worldwide indicators—economic opportunity, political power, education, and health—according to the World Economic Forum's Global Gender Gap Report. The report examines data from 156 countries and has used the same methodology for 15 years. The gap grew by 36 years in the last 12 months, the largest yearly increase since the report started. While there has been progress in education and health, there has been a decline in women's political power and economic opportunity. It will be an average of 267 years before the wage gap closes worldwide and women have economic equality with men.

No country has achieved gender equality. The Nordic countries of Iceland, Finland, and Norway are the top performers, and Iceland took the top spot for the twelfth year. New Zealand was in the fourth spot. The United States rose 23 places in the rankings to 30th place due to increasing women's political empowerment. Western Europe was the best-performing region. The Middle East and North Africa region has the largest gender gap due to only 31 percent of women participating in the labor force.

Discrimination, one of the four outcomes of sexism, is the unjust and prejudicial treatment of women. Discrimination against women has created the 135-year gap in parity between women and men. Discrimination, making unjustified distinctions between people, happens in countries with and without laws against it. Many types of discrimination, often referred to as informal discrimination, happen outside of the jurisdiction of the law. Discrimination against women can be caused by the sexist biases people have and usually starts with prejudices and stereotypes in the form of microaggression. When society accepts sexist microaggressions, they can escalate and turn into acts of discrimination against women.

FOUR OUTCOMES OF SEXISM	
Microaggression	Discrimination
Sexist Language	Education
Stereotypes	Employment
Objectification	Wage Gap
Shaming	Career
Mansplaining	Healthcare
Invalidation	Sexual
Harassment	Violence
Verbal	Physical
Physical	Sexual
Online	Emotional
Bullying	Economic
Street	Coercive Control
Flashing	Femicide

Six Types of Discrimination

Women experience discrimination in ways that have a significant impact on their ability to achieve equality with men. Six types of discrimination that directly relate to the World Economic Forum's Report indicators are education, employment, wage gap, career, healthcare, and sexual. The education of girls and women has the most significant impact on advancing gender equality worldwide.

Yet, many girls are intentionally not provided with the opportunity for an education. Even when women have educational opportunities, discriminatory practices in the workforce affect employment and create a wage gap. In many cases, women don't receive the career opportunities that men do, and their advancement is limited. Often, women worldwide don't have access to healthcare or get their needs addressed appropriately. How a woman expresses her sexuality and sexual preferences can trigger biases that lead to discrimination.

After college, while I was working at a local bank, my boss gave notice, and they posted his position. Another female colleague and I decided to use our education and skills and applied. The hiring manager, a male vice president, heard we were applying and said to me, "Well, I don't think either of you should bother; you are not qualified for the job." In anger, I called human resources to ask how he could say I shouldn't bother to apply when I met all the requirements. Suddenly, my colleague and I were informed we had an interview. It was a "courtesy" interview that human resources told him he had to do. Neither of us got a second interview, and they hired a man for the job. They even paid to move him from another state. I left not long after that—both the job and the banking industry.
—Deanna, United States

Education

Girls' education opens doors to good job opportunities and access to financial resources. Education provides them with important information about their rights and the confidence to speak up for themselves. Surveys in 55 developing countries reveal that girls are more likely to be out of school at a much earlier age than boys. The education of girls and women can lead to improved maternal health and reduced infant mortality. Children of mothers with secondary education or higher are twice as likely to survive beyond age five than those whose mothers have no education.

Every additional year of primary school increases girls' eventual wages by 10 to 20 percent. It also encourages them to marry later and have fewer children, making them less vulnerable to violence. The only way for women to achieve equality is for gender parity to exist in educational systems. Yet, more than 130 million girls worldwide are not in school. Almost two-thirds of the world's 775 million illiterate adults are women.

Girls that can attend school are often underestimated and experience discrimination. From the time they enter kindergarten, they are instilled with the belief that they are less talented than their male peers. Research studies found that girls encounter sexism at school that impacts their confidence. The textbooks may not promote positive stereotypes or include women's accomplishments. Assumptions are made that girls want to read or play hopscotch and boys want to build or play sports. Boys are often made the leaders of team activities and are called on more frequently. Guest speakers, class activities, and books selected to read are usually chosen based on the boys' interests. Many school dress codes are sexist and discriminatory.

Girls interested in science, technology, engineering, and medicine (STEM) may be discouraged if others say such topics aren't feminine pursuits. College-bound women are less likely to enter STEM or other traditionally male fields because of discrimination. Microaggression thrives in schools at all levels: primary, secondary, university, and graduate programs. Teachers and students bring their implicit and explicit biases to school through microaggressions that lead to discrimination. Because of sexism, educational institutions with well-intentioned educators reinforce barriers for girls and women.

> *Shortly before graduating from my university, I started interviewing with recruiters who frequently asked if I had a boyfriend and planned to give up my job when I got married or pregnant. I didn't even realize that these questions were discriminatory. I thought all female students got asked these questions. When I talked with some alumnae, they told me that I would have no option but to stop working after having a child. They said that having children is the main contribution women make to Japanese society. Now that I'm working, I realize that many women don't return to work after giving birth. I'm not willing to give up my career aspirations to have a family.*
>
> —Hana, Japan

Employment

Men dominated the workforce for many years, and sexism is built into the workplace. Most employment practices were designed with men in mind and can discriminate against women. Job advertisements for more traditionally male roles, including those in science, technology, engineering, and medicine, tend to have more masculine words and discourage women from applying. The text can be sexist.

Creating a slate of candidates for a role perceived as traditionally masculine can be biased toward male candidates, including managerial and executive positions. A focus on creating a slate of candidates with half of them being women is often not considered a priority. Sexism sneaks into interviews in various ways, and stereotypes are prevalent. Interviewers may wonder if a woman will get pregnant and leave the job or won't be able to work as many hours or travel if she has children. Interviewers can have implicit or explicit biases about a woman in any role.

Employment discrimination toward women is built into economic systems worldwide. When a crisis like the pandemic strikes, women are hit harder economically. They tend to earn less and save less, are the majority of single-parent households, and hold more insecure jobs. They have less access to social support systems. Therefore, women are less able to absorb the economic shocks than men. For many women, school closures and social distancing measures increased their unpaid care, making them less able to take on or balance paid work.

Unpaid care is considered women's work and is a universal issue caused by sexism. Women carry out at least two and a half times more unpaid household and care work than men. One study showed that worldwide, women spend an average of three to six hours a day on unpaid care, while men spend between half an hour and two hours a day. Unpaid care becomes a vicious cycle for women that keeps them earning less and saving less.

A coworker and I were appointed as co-managers over the operations of a local quasi-government entity. I was to run the office administration functions and he was to run operations. He made $20k a year more than me. I questioned it, and they said he had more experience in his field. I replied that I had equivalent experience in my field. I was then told he'd been with the company longer. But, they said, they would give me a raise. They did. They also gave him a raise. Each year, my pay increased, but so did his. By the time I left the position 15 *years later, he made about $40k a year more than me. The pay gap widened. But like many, I needed the job and didn't make waves. I should have.*

—Sorcha, United States

Wage Gap

The wage gap between men and women is a worldwide issue linked to discriminatory practices. It could take an average of 267 years before the wage gap closes and women receive the same salary as men for similar work. The wage gap varies by country, race, and ethnicity. Women workers make less than men in all countries, across all sectors, for all levels of education, and in all age groups. Globally, women earn 77 cents for every dollar men make for work of equal value—with an even wider wage gap for women with children.

In the United States, women on average earned 83 cents for every dollar a man earned. Black women earned 64 cents, Hispanic women 57 cents, and Native American women 60 cents for every dollar a non-Hispanic white man made in the United States. The intersection of sexism with racism impacts women of color. In the United Kingdom, the gender pay gap has widened despite efforts to address the gap. Women were paid 87p for every pound paid to men. Australia's national gender pay gap was 14.2 percent. On average, women in Australia earn $261.50 less per week than men. One of the reasons for the global pay gap is that women are underrepresented in higher-level management, such as senior or middle management roles. The many factors contributing to the gender wage gap, including types of jobs, hours worked, and salary earned, can be directly and indirectly influenced by sexism and discrimination.

Women's internalized sexism, beliefs about themselves caused by sexist experiences can affect their employment and earning opportunities. Research has shown that women are less likely to apply for more senior jobs than their current position. They often won't apply for a new role unless they feel highly qualified for the job.

When women negotiate for a higher salary, they are three times as likely not to reach an agreement as men with a similar offer. Women don't need negotiation training; they need to unlearn the sexist biases they have absorbed since childhood that impact their beliefs on women's behaviors. Similarly, internalized sexism causes imposter syndrome. Since their youth, the sexist experiences women have had tell them they aren't good enough.

The research found that women ask for raises as often as men, but men are more successful in their requests, with a success rate of 15 percent for women and 20 percent for men. Girls learn that they are expected to follow the rules and do as they are told at a very young age. Women who negotiate aggressively can face a backlash linked to a likeability factor. When women negotiate, they aren't behaving as stereotypical females. People think they are pushy and aggressive and like them less, which results in women not getting the job, promotion, or raise.

> *Looking back on my 32-year career in engineering and sales, I now see how women receive assignments with less opportunity to succeed financially. A branch manager decides who gets assigned what customers and how branch quotas are distributed. In the good old boy network, men get the best accounts and achievable quotas. Women receive accounts that are less likely to do well and quotas that are often unachievable. If women are to succeed in these environments, they have to work twice as hard to generate sales. Women often don't meet their quotas and therefore don't earn a full salary and bonus.*
> **—Sheila, United States**

Career

Many aspects of a woman's career are affected by discrimination, including performance management reviews, promotions, and job reductions. The performance review process in organizations is subjective and research has shown that sexism causes women to receive biased reviews. A study using content analysis of reviews showed that women were 1.4 times more likely to receive critical subjective feedback than positive or critical objective feedback.

Sexist biases that invade the performance review process lead to double standards. The same behaviors will get a negative spin in a woman's review and a positive spin in a man's review. An employee performance issue related to confidence in working with clients was described as "shrinking" and "a lack of confidence" in a woman's review. In the man's review, he was described as "needing to develop his natural ability to work with people."

In another example of comparable reviews, the woman was described as having "analysis paralysis," and the man was described as "having careful thoughtfulness." Women get less constructive feedback, and their performance is more likely to be attributed to things like luck and working long hours rather than skills and abilities. One study found that the common words used in women's performance reviews were abrasive, bossy, aggressive, strident, and emotional. Out of those words, "aggressive" was only used occasionally to describe men. These are examples of sexist microaggression in action. When microaggression goes unchecked, it turns into discrimination and impacts women's performance review ratings, salary, and opportunities for advancement.

The number of women in companies tends to average around 50 percent at the non-managerial level. The number of women in supervisor, manager, and executive levels gets significantly smaller at each progressively senior level. Discriminatory performance review and selection processes contribute to the dwindling number of women in leadership roles.

In the United States, one study found that for every 100 men promoted to manager, only 86 women were promoted, which reduces the number of women in the pipeline for higher positions. There is a persistent lack of women in leadership positions, with women representing just 27 percent of all manager positions globally, almost the same proportion as in 1995, and women of color are significantly underrepresented within that percentage. Compared to men, women spend substantial time on diversity, equity, and inclusion work that is often unrecognized "unpaid" work.

Discriminatory practices can be found in succession planning and how successors are identified for senior-level roles in a company. A succession process typically uses performance review data along with potential data. The performance review data may already be biased against women, and potential data tends to be a list of competencies that can be subjective and can incorporate biases when rated.

Only 18 percent of enterprises surveyed by the United Nations had a female chief executive officer. In the Fortune 500, there were only 37 female chief executive officers. Often performance review data is one of the criteria for selection when a company goes through a reduction in force (RIF). Women who receive biased performance reviews could be adversely impacted during a RIF. Women's careers are filled with discrimination barriers that lead to stationary or backward movement rather than forward movement.

Discrimination at work has negative consequences for women and organizations. A study conducted by Speak Out Revolution reported that 85 percent of women experienced a negative impact on their mental health, 83 percent experienced a negative effect on their confidence, and 81 percent wanted to leave their organization after being subjected to unfair treatment.

After spending a year seconded to my company's executive team, I was given a growth assignment to lead a significant new portfolio. My boss (male) had difficulties leading his teams and was struggling to operate. After I made multiple attempts to help him, including building executive oversight support, he attempted to manage me out. His justification was that I was too "directive" and needed to know my place. I am confident that, had I been male, showing this initiative and leadership would not have resulted in a (failed) attempt at retaliatory dismissal.

—**Marcy, Canada**

Healthcare

Many women believe the healthcare industry fails to address their needs appropriately and that sexism plays a role. One study revealed that 52 percent of women believe that sexist discrimination negatively affects their medical care. Women feel challenged to prove that their symptoms and pain levels are real. The difference is even more significant when the patient is a woman of color.

Women are typically diagnosed later than men—2.5 years later for cancer and 4.5 years later for diabetes. Research indicates 700 diseases in which women have been diagnosed later than men. A Canadian study of 1.3 million patients showed that women a male surgeon operates on are 15 percent more likely to suffer a bad outcome and 32 percent more likely to die than if a woman operates on them. The healthcare industry is failing women with adverse and sometimes deadly consequences.

Throughout history, women have been excluded from clinical trials simply because they were women. This exclusion from the research has translated to less insight into women's responses to illnesses. When women's physical reactions to illness fail to align with the male indicators, women often refuse the diagnosis. When that happens, they are diagnosed as emotional and hysterical, when a man refusing a diagnosis would be considered confident. Doctors then suggest that the symptoms are all in the woman's head, that she has mental health problems, and conduct no further testing. Once again, sexist microaggression unchecked turns into discrimination, this time with potentially deadly results.

Sexist discrimination exists in all areas specific to women's reproductive health. On any day, 800 million people worldwide have their period, and an average woman spends 3,000 days of her life menstruating. The cost of menstrual hygiene products isn't affordable to many. Contraception is frequently unavailable for the women who need it. Menopausal therapies can be expensive and difficult to obtain. Often even talking about such topics is considered taboo.

The lack of contraception and abortion healthcare leads to unwanted pregnancies and maternal mortality. The United States experienced 660 maternal deaths in one year. The maternal death rate for Black women in the United States is 2.5 times the ratio for white women. The lack of access to reproductive healthcare is a discriminatory barrier that makes it difficult for women and girls worldwide to reach their social and economic potential.

My boss shared that she wished she could only work with men. When she had the opportunity, she began mainly hiring men. She eventually promoted two men above me, though neither was qualified or experienced. She was aware others didn't agree with her, and she created an environment that excluded others. It could be described as hostile. As a single mom, I wanted to avoid retaliation, as the job paid well for the area, and I loved my actual role. I felt like my mistakes were used as examples to make me look foolish to my internal team. She and her "male

team" embellished things about my personal life. I kept my
head down, did my best to be a helpful teammate, and focused
on being a trusted partner to my customers. After she was let
go, a few people confirmed that these things were true. Again,
the fear of losing my job kept me from taking much action.
                                        —Kathy, United States

Sexual

The sexualization of women and girls contributes to sexist biases and discrimination in all walks of life. A woman's perceived value often comes from her sexual appeal to the exclusion of other characteristics. Women are frequently held to an unrealistic standard of physical attractiveness propagated by the media in magazines, advertisements, television shows, movies, and social media. In sports, women are judged on their perceived femininity and required to wear revealing uniforms when they should be evaluated for their athleticism. Women are penalized for dressing "too sexy" or "too conservative" at school and work. Women grow up knowing they are constantly being evaluated on their looks and stereotypical womanness.

Women receive criticism about their appearance daily from both men and women and get slotted into roles based on people's perceptions. Men are not subjected to the same evaluation process. When women don't meet the stereotypical expectations of how a woman should look and act, they can experience discrimination on and off the job. And power is at the root of it all, as it is with most sexist behaviors. Reducing a woman's worth to stereotypical beliefs about her womanness diminishes her value.

Lesbian, bisexual, and trans women often don't fit the stereotype of the heterosexual female and can face additional sexist discrimination. According to the Women in the Workplace report, lesbian and bisexual women face disrespectful behavior in their workplaces. They are more likely than women overall to experience microaggression, including being interrupted, having their judgment questioned, and being expected to speak on behalf of all people with their identity.

These women hear more negative feedback about how they present themselves at work, such as being told that they are too outspoken and confrontational. They don't feel comfortable talking about their personal lives and sharing challenges or experiences of burnout with colleagues. They are usually the only person of their sexuality at the workplace and often feel isolated and scrutinized.

A McKinsey report indicates that many trans women don't feel comfortable being out at work because their gender identity doesn't conform to sexist stereotypes. They feel less supported by their managers in the workplace and find it's hard to get promoted. Trans women feel socially devalued, which provides the basis for discrimination. They find interactions with coworkers very difficult and frequently leave jobs due to hostility and discrimination. As long as the value of women and girls comes from their stereotypical womanness, women who self-identify as women or are perceived to be women will continue to experience sexual discrimination.

> *Last year I finally decided I was comfortable enough to come out to one of my coworkers. When I told her that I'm a lesbian and I'm married to a woman, she said, "I don't think you should tell your manager, because he's homophobic. He does not believe in gay marriage. He will treat you differently, and it could impact your performance reviews and opportunities for promotion." After that conversation, I have kept my personal life private. It's hard keeping it a secret and not bringing my whole self to work. It's like living two separate lives.*
>
> **—Jill, England**

Challenge Sexism, Champion Women's Rights, and Create Equality

Following is a list of actions that men and women can take to stop sexist discrimination and be antisexist. Review the list and add items to your Antisexist Action Plan.

- Review the six types of discrimination; education, employment, wage gap, career, healthcare, and sexual. Select a category that is more relevant and important to you than the others.
- Write down the types of sexism you have personally experienced or have seen others experience within that category of discrimination. Determine one or two actions to challenge sexist discrimination in the category you selected.
- List one or two actions you can take to champion women's rights related to your selected category. This may involve changing policy, practices, programs, or laws within an organization or region, or becoming a volunteer with an activist group.
- Select one of the six categories where you have expressed sexist biases. Write down your examples and determine one or two actions to take to help you manage your sexism and become antisexist.
- Identify people you could talk to about their experiences of discrimination within any of the six categories of discrimination. Talking with and listening to others is an excellent way to learn more about sexism and being antisexist.
- If you know that discrimination is happening to someone, be an ally and speak up. Intervene as appropriate by talking to the individual or other involved parties.

Discrimination is against the law in many countries. If you are woman experiencing sexist discrimination here are some steps to take.

- Focus on specific issues, facts and details. Remove the emotion.
- Keep documentation and make a record of the offensive actions.
- Talk with the person in charge about your issues and see if they can be resolved.
- Report the discrimination to human resources or management.
- Be aware that retaliation for filing a complaint may take place. If you experience retaliation document it.
- If you have complained about the discrimination and haven't gotten a response you may want to talk with an attorney.

SEVEN

Enough

By Izmira Santiago-Mikel

You alone are enough. You have nothing to prove to anybody.

—MAYA ANGELOU

a·dapt

/ə'dapt/

verb

make (something) suitable for a new use or purpose; modify.
Similar: alter/ make alterations to/ change/ adjust/ make adjustments
to/ convert/ transform/ redesign/ restyle/ refashion/ remodel/ reshape/
revamp/ rework/ redo/ reconstruct/ reorganize/ customize/ tailor/
improve/ make improvements to/ amend/ refine/ tweak
Conform.

A swift Google search will straightforwardly reveal what it means
to adapt. In many ways, it is seen as a positive outcome. To me,
and to many like me, it was the equivalent of not only conditioning
myself to a new culture, but also shedding any true sense of who I

was in the process.

I was born and raised in a small sub-continental piece of land surrounded by stunning shores and the hopes of American dreams. Where English was a second language and our identities were in many ways skewed by the vast external influences that ultimately made us who we are. The women belonged in the kitchen, and not to themselves. The men had all the liberties that we as women fancied. Both sides would act as if the opportunities and responsibilities were equitable.

Truth is, the traditional gender roles have always been deeply entrenched in our culture. I still had the opportunity and privilege to be raised by a somewhat progressive family, where the women are responsible for creating their own path. My mother is very much a feminist and taught me about powerful women in history and how I could be like them. However, there were still unspoken rules and agreements on how to adequately present yourself in light of being a willing and active participant in the patriarchal culture that bounded us. Sadly, I would often stumble and perpetuate this conundrum by falsely comporting myself as an equal at school, at work, and in my relationships; I was preaching feminism, but subconsciously the voice I heard inside my head said, "You're independent, but know your place."

Fast-forward to adulthood. After graduating college, I worked at a couple of companies and landed reputable roles with lofty salaries but no clear path to a future. So, I decided to apply for my dream job, and to my surprise, they scheduled an interview. After what seemed like endless interviews, they called back. I could hardly believe what I was hearing. It was 2010, and I had just received what I considered the opportunity of a lifetime. I landed my dream job at a massive private philanthropy and accepted the position. Without knowing much about what awaited me, I moved across the country in hopes of building a great career for myself. While this was not my first job, it was certainly the one job I desperately wanted.

The woman that hired me as her assistant had the wisdom and

exquisite beauty that I'd only read about in poetic renditions. She had a kind heart, a lovely spirit, and for some odd reason chose to take a chance and give me the opportunity. During our interviews, I remember thinking to myself, *This is the type of woman I strive to be.* She was a confident, warm, articulate, well-dressed woman of color. All the things I was not, as a woman of color myself, or at least didn't consider myself to be at the time.

She and the team I was working for decided to bring in an external coach to help with our interpersonal dynamics. He interviewed us all, created trainings, helped us workshop through some of our problem areas, and provided some additional one-on-one time for team members that wanted help with envisioning and illustrating their career path. In my own open ambitions to become a leader in my newfound field, I asked my supervisor if I could request one of the available coaching sessions. Without hesitation, she smiled and said yes.

The coach sat down quietly and read through his assessment. As I waited patiently, he took a deep breath and proceeded to provide his feedback. "Iz … may I call you that? I'm not sure how to pronounce your name." He tried again. "Es … Es … I like Iz better." Before I could even respond, correct him, and decline his request to use a pet name, he leaned in. "Iz, it's your accent, your hair, and your hoop earrings; it's just all so ethnic." He paused. "You must understand that as a woman, you can't allow yourself such freedoms if you want to be successful in this environment. If your desire is to launch your career to its full potential, you will have to make some drastic changes."

It was clear to me that this person wouldn't understand the need to unpack how sexist and racist those comments were. His limited understanding suggested that being able to be that "free" with my appearance and communication style would only be acceptable if I were a man, a white man at that. I was floored. I couldn't understand how much more I could adapt to this patriarchal, white supremacist environment without completely losing myself. Was it even possible? If I did in fact change, would I be a part of the club?

I tried, and it seemed to work. Every day I would walk into the office projecting the persona of women and men I pretended to be, because being myself was seemingly not an option. I then started to acquiesce into playing the roles assigned to me. I did an extraordinary job at remaining quiet and would effortlessly disappear into the background. I would then desperately seek to learn their expectations of who I should be. And even though I learned how to play the part, I was constantly protecting myself from their gendered comments and racial microaggressions. I'd go on like this for a couple of years. I started to use their words and their mannerisms. I would dress the way they dressed and read the books they read.

I craved the days when being different was celebrated. When I could wear flamboyant garb, allow my hair to be wild and curly, and be measured by my knowledge and skill, not by my accent and appearance. A place where I didn't have unreasonable standards of beauty and femininity forced on me, or on the contrary, have to deny said femininity in a world that tells you to be more like a man.

Smile, but not too big, because it may be misconstrued as flirting. You must be attractive, but not too visible; they won't take you seriously. Be assertive but not outspoken; no one likes a woman that talks too much. Have an opinion, but only if it's agreeable; avoid giving the impression that you're angry or hard to work with.

One morning I woke up and started getting ready for work. I had a big presentation that day and had previously chosen a black tailored power suit and heavily starched white button-down shirt. I stared at it intently. Something was missing, and I couldn't figure out what it was. I continued my morning schedule, and while preparing breakfast, it hit me. I missed home. I missed my mom.

I remembered how she filled a room with her laughter and how she always voiced her opinion. She was strong, she wore red lipstick, she was always unapologetically herself. How disappointed would she be if she knew what was really going on? If she learned how far I'd come to just become a muted version of myself? I walked into my living room and turned on music she loved. We would listen to these songs of protest and celebration when I was a child. I marched to my closet and chose instead to wear a bright red A-line dress she gifted me a year before. I let my curls out and wrapped my hair up in a lovely silk scarf she and my father brought back from one of their visits to our island. I felt better already.

I walked to work determined. I was prepared to deliver and felt confident about the work. I entered the office and followed my usual routine. I docked my laptop and went to the common kitchen to grab some tea while my computer powered up.

A white, male, higher-up co-worker walks by and says, "Well, good morning! Como esta? You are looking very 'la isla bonita' today. Are you ready for your presentation, señorita?" I frustratingly nod my head. He goes on, "You know, I think you should let me do the external partners portion of the presentation; we want to make sure they know how serious we are about the work. I don't know if they'll be able to focus with such a sexy Latina in the room."

Everyone has a tipping point; I'd just reached mine. In a slightly raised tone and with intense pitch I exclaimed, "Enough! Please, refrain from using sexist and racist comments in my presence. Just, ENOUGH." Shocked, he paused as if I had just lost my mind and replied, "Gosh, it was just a compliment. I'm very much a feminist!" I was certain I would lose my job that day but felt the responsibility of standing up for myself and others like me experiencing the same dynamic in the workplace.

So, I regrouped and calmly responded, "If I may speak freely and provide you with some feedback. Women constantly face the reinforced expectation of attaining and preserving an attractive physical appearance. This perpetuates archaic philosophies of a woman's worth being primarily associated with her looks. Furthermore, attempting to change our appearance so it fits in with the Euro-centric, male-centered constructs of what a professional woman should look, act, or sound like is against the feminist agenda. In many cases, similarly facing objectification and having our contributions and capabilities dismissed based on physical appearance is also against the feminist agenda."

He listened. He apologized. Did it change anything? Frankly, I don't know. I can't say if it did or didn't for him. What I can say is that was the day I realized two extremely necessary things about myself. I'd had enough. I was enough. There are five key lessons I've learned on my journey to realizing I'm enough.

- Being your authentic self is a choice. The option exists to use uncomfortable situations as learning opportunities. The people around you will either adapt and accept you for who you are and in turn invite your perspective or the situation will compel you to find a healthier dynamic where your influence is not only included but appreciated.
- Speak up. The price of fear and insecurity is exceedingly high.
- Don't settle. Get clear on what matters to you and stay committed to that vision.
- Be willing to risk the usual. If the opportunity doesn't exist, create it for yourself.
- Continue to grow. Your fundamental upbringing doesn't mean your perspectives are set in stone. There is nothing wrong with adapting. Albert Einstein said, "The measure of intelligence is the ability to change." Understand the difference between being flexible and compromising yourself.

Biography

With true understanding of education's power to uplift, Izmira Santiago-Mikel has dedicated her career to promoting causes that seek to open doors for all, focusing on underrepresented populations throughout the United States and Puerto Rico. With over a decade of experience in philanthropy management across a variety of sectors, Izmira serves as CEO and Founder of Stakeholders Collective. Izmira was born and raised in Puerto Rico. Her parents placed high value on education and were part of the Young Lords, an organization championing human rights, education, and community programs. Izmira studied music and sound engineering in college and went on to earn her MBA. She currently lives in Washington, DC, with her husband Eli and young son Miles. Izmira serves on the Advisory Board of Directors for Friends of Puerto Rico, a social impact organization based in Washington, DC.

EIGHT

Embracing My Trueness
Cheryl Horvath

*A strong woman loves, forgives, walks away, lets go, tries again, and
perseveres ... no matter what life throws at her.*

—Unknown

It was a scary idea, and even scarier to imagine following through
with it. "It" was a request from a woman's professional networking
group to be a featured speaker at our annual retreat. Keep in mind this
was a group of 100-plus influential women from across a metro area, all
leaders in their businesses, nonprofits, and professional organizations.

Members included doctors, the county attorney, president of the
largest real estate company both locally and statewide, small- and
large-business owners who also maintained leadership positions in the
city's various leadership councils and boards, and top administrators
in county and city governments. A hundred women considered to be
at the top of their respective fields. I was a member by virtue of my
status within my county fire district as the top woman chief officer.
And I was being invited to talk with this intimidating group about

vulnerability. I was terrified.

The women in my networking group would laugh if they knew how terrified I was to share my story. They would laugh because I am a firefighter, and in their eyes, a woman of courage. Firefighters run into burning buildings and danger when most people are running out. I learned to suppress feelings and emotion, especially as a woman in public safety. The last thing I needed to do around the guys was to show emotion and be perceived as weak. I needed to be strong, capable, and part of the group, not separating myself because I was a woman. And that is what my breakfast club members saw—strength, not fear. If they only knew.

I was given two months to prepare for the retreat and encouraged to focus on my story. The friend who threw me under the bus and offered my name to the retreat planning committee was a woman I had shared deep conversations with about both my personal and professional life. She is a strategic planning consultant and has a brilliant mind, very successful in her field and considered one of the leaders in our city until she relocated to be with her new husband. We had developed a special bond over the years, as unlikely as that was, coming from vastly different backgrounds and working in dissimilar work environments. But she was the one who knew how to challenge me, and speaking at the retreat was no exception. I took the bait.

Vulnerability to me only meant one thing: time to get personal, which was not at all an arena I was comfortable with. I pondered the topic for weeks, trying to decide what my story was to tell. I settled on something that had been a part of my life for so many years but had remained hidden and unspoken professionally, mostly by me.

A part of me that had hardened over time to the point where its own compartment was more robust than any other compartment in my life. It was impenetrable, or at least I thought so. As I explored the reasons why this part of me had become so invincible, I realized the effort I had put forth over the years to protect this part of me was all-consuming and exhausting. And I was good at protecting this part of me, separating it from co-workers as if I were two completely different people, the Cheryl at work and the Cheryl at home.

I chose to talk with the group of power gals at the retreat about my lifestyle, my sexual preference for women, and how I had become an expert in living two lives, one at home and one at work. It's nice to think that we can be accepted for who we are by everyone we meet, but the reality is that is not true.

Women in nontraditional work environments already have enough stacked against them when we choose to enter professions like the fire service. Less than 4 percent of the paid professional firefighting force in the United States is made up of women, the lowest percentage of women in any of the uniformed services, including the Marine Corps. Add the need to excel to the point of overperformance just to achieve acceptance, and it's apparent that being a lesbian is not exactly the frosting on the cake for a woman in a nontraditional field trying to make her way.

At the retreat I shared the story of my upbringing and being raised Catholic. Going to church every Sunday and always trying to be good. I talked about my need to constantly do the right thing throughout my life, not making anyone else uncomfortable, even if it meant denying myself that same happiness.

I talked about my family, specifically my parents, and the difficulty of trying to talk with my mother about my lifestyle. She and my father were of the generation that does not like to talk about difficult topics, period. When my oldest brother decided to drop a bomb on my parents about my lifestyle, my mother panicked because she already knew, as I had tried to talk to her, but had not told my father. And my father was furious. Everywhere I turned, there were minefields to avoid when it came to my lifestyle, and I was an expert at dancing through minefields. But it took a lot out of me. It is like situational awareness on steroids.

Sure, I had plenty of friends and what appeared to be a happy life. I was also an expert in not talking about or sharing my personal life at work. It was not all bad. I had people throughout my life at work who I could confide in, but in general, to be able to declare myself open and out at work was not a tool I had in my toolbox. It wasn't like I wanted to throw rainbows up in my office at work, but it would have been nice to at least *talk* about putting rainbows up in my office. I constantly sought to do the right thing in every situation, which meant I veiled my lifestyle and carried that burden for years.

My life came tumbling down when I decided to leave a long-term relationship with another woman. I literally packed a bag, dropped my then 11-year-old daughter at her friend's house for a sleepover, and walked away from my personal life. I knew that I was hurting someone else, but could no longer live a lie of not being happy. It would be unfair to blame the unhappiness on one person.

It was a lifetime of carrying the burden of denial that was weighing me down, trying to do the right thing all the time, and my desire and understanding for love was simply gone. That is when I leaned on my friend, the strategic planner, the woman who would provide me with shelter, forgiveness, and long talks to help heal my pain, my anger at myself, and allow me to be me. Her grace during that time was remarkable.

I cried as I shared my story at the retreat. Other women in the room cried as well, quite a few, which gave me incredible strength. I ended my story by sharing the happiness of my newfound love and our plans to wed four months later, now that same-sex marriage was legal in our state. We were planning a huge wedding with 160 people, some of whom I worked with at the time. And my 85-year-old mother and 18-year-old daughter would walk me down the aisle. I shared my realization that being happy meant holding my now wife's hand as we walked down the street regardless of who is watching us, and frankly, not caring what anyone else thinks. It sounds easy to do, but it took me 56 years of life to get there.

Age certainly gives one the sense that we have gained some wisdom. That may not be accurate or even reliable, but what I know and have learned up to this point in my life makes me feel like it is worth sharing as a part of my continuing story.

- Be gracious to yourself and others. Allow yourself to be happy, while also allowing others around you to accept who you are at their pace and in their own time. Maybe it is easier for me to see this now since I do not really care what people think of me or my lifestyle anymore. But deep down, I do want them to care, because there will be other people they come across who will be different from them. I always desire for the road to be smoother for others who come after me, and part of that is recognizing new perspectives and helping others do the same.
- Speak your truth, whatever that is. Advice like this is contextual, but the point is to be yourself. Year and years of suppressing my full lifestyle resulted in nothing more than a huge burden for me and fractured relationships. It is tough when you know your truth may hurt family members or loved ones, or create a wedge between co-workers, but we cannot make life easy on everyone else and ignore our own happiness. My parents eventually came around, and we enjoyed a very special relationship until they passed away. It was so hard and so emotional, but the relationship afterwards was exponentially more meaningful because we could all be truthful with each other. Interestingly enough, when I turned the focus on my family, close friends, and our relationships, nothing else mattered to me.
- Believe in yourself and believe in others. My parents, particularly my father, told me and taught me that I could do anything I put my mind to. That is where I gained my strength to become a firefighter. I try to pass that along to my daughter so that

she embraces confidence and allows it to guide her in her life. I definitely would not be where I am today, a fire chief, if I listened to the naysayers and allowed them to block my path.

- Do not be afraid to tell your story. I learned so much from the experience of sharing my vulnerability at the networking retreat. It has made me a better person, a more compassionate leader, and hopefully more relatable as a fire chief. Public safety is a difficult work environment for women as we try to navigate exercising our leadership and deal with all the biases that exist in the workplace, both from men and other women. Too often I would show a strong demeanor when being more vulnerable would probably have been the better path forward. What we have to realize as women, similar to my personal experience, is that the naysayers exist regardless of what you do. If we try to navigate the naysayers (i.e., do the right thing), we deny ourselves the opportunity for deep, meaningful relationships in all parts of our lives.

- Have a tribe of women you can rely on, fall back on, and give your support to when necessary. The networking group I belonged to was a huge part of my life during a difficult period of transition. Had I not made the choice to be a part of that group, I would not be where I am today, both personally and professionally.

Biography

Cheryl Horvath is a fire chief and longtime advocate for women in the fire service. She co-founded a public safety camp for high school girls to encourage young women to consider a career in public safety. Cheryl is married and enjoys spending time with family and friends.

NINE

Four Outcomes of Sexism: Harassment

If you see harassment happening, speak up. Being harassed is terrible; having bystanders pretend they don't notice is infinitely worse.

—CELESTE NG

When microaggression, in the form of locker-room banter, becomes normalized, men get to hide their misogyny behind sexist jokes. Accepting "boys will boys" behavior expressed through demeaning jokes and remarks about women allows microaggression to escalate to harassment and violence. The police officer who murdered Sarah Everard in England made female officers uncomfortable. Instead of speaking up and reporting his harassing behavior, his male colleagues nicknamed him "the rapist." Sarah's killer was accused of indecent exposure several times before Sarah's kidnap, rape, and murder. His sexist behavior and harassment of women were accepted and encouraged by male colleagues.

Harassment, one of the four outcomes of sexism, is behavior that intimidates, demeans, humiliates, or embarrasses women and is disturbing, upsetting, or threatening. When microaggression goes unchecked, it can escalate to harassment. Sexist harassment is typically committed by men against women. It usually has a sexual component, though it can be strictly based on gender biases.

Many countries have laws against some types of harassment. In the United States, sexual harassment in employment discrimination becomes unlawful when enduring offensive conduct becomes a condition of employment or when the behavior is severe enough to create a hostile work environment. Worldwide there are no legal impacts for many kinds of harassment. Sexual harassment often goes unreported, and the harassers go unpunished.

A study of women in the United States conducted by Stop Street Harassment found that 81 percent of women had experienced some form of sexual harassment in their lifetime. The results showed that 77 percent of women had experienced verbal sexual harassment, and 51 percent had been touched sexually without their permission. Online sexual harassment had impacted 41 percent of women, and 66 percent had been sexually harassed in public. Approximately one-third of the women had experienced unwanted genital flashing.

Sexual harassment can cause women to feel anxious and depressed, similar to victims of sexual violence, and force them to change their job, residence, and routine to avoid the harassment. Only 10 percent had filed a report with the authorities. Because women don't even mention it to friends or family, sexual harassment is allowed to thrive because of women's silence, and men get to escape without consequences.

FOUR OUTCOMES OF SEXISM	
Microaggression	**Discrimination**
Sexist Language	Education
Stereotypes	Employment
Objectification	Wage Gap
Shaming	Career
Mansplaining	Healthcare
Invalidation	Sexual
Harassment	**Violence**
Verbal	Physical
Physical	Sexual
Online	Emotional
Bullying	Economic
Street	Coercive Control
Flashing	Femicide

Six Types of Harassment

As with all of the four outcomes of sexism, harassment is about power and control; only in the case of harassment sexism has escalated to become more demeaning, intimidating, and frightening to women. Women experience various types of harassment, and all have a detrimental impact on their lives. The six types of harassment that frequently occur are verbal, physical, online, bullying, street, and flashing. Verbal harassment is hostile or offensive speech, oral, written, or visual. Physical harassment is when a man inappropriately touches a woman against her will.

Online harassment includes being called offensive names, purposefully embarrassed, physically threatened, stalked, or sexually harassed. Bullying is a pattern of repeatedly and deliberately harming and humiliating girls more vulnerable than the bully. Street harassment includes unwanted comments, gestures, or acts directed at women in a public space without their consent. Flashing happens when a man exposes his genitals to a woman, typically in public. Most of the behaviors in the harassment category are sexually related. However, some might be gender-based negative comments or jokes.

> *I experienced sexism at work in my first full-time job in the automotive industry. I heard many sexist comments about my body, looks, and clothes working in human resources. Comments were also made about me not being smart enough to understand technical matters. Lots of sexist jokes were told about women who were destined to be housewives and take care of numerous kids. "Why do women have smaller feet? To be able to stand closer to the sink." These comments were not only made by my coworkers but also by the CEO of the company. Being a young woman at the beginning of my career, I was humiliated, misjudged, snubbed, and degraded numerous times. It made me feel like I should hate men for their sexist behavior.*
>
> **—Kasia, Poland**

Verbal

Verbal harassment is hostile or offensive speech—oral, written, or visual. It is microaggression escalating to harassment. It's probably the most common form of harassment both off and on the job. Three-quarters of women surveyed indicated they had experienced verbal harassment. People often find it challenging to identify because of different reactions from people. It includes making inappropriate jokes, remarks, teasing, or asking sexually related questions and requesting dates; unwelcome sexual advances, and making inappropriate sounds like kissing or whistling fall within this category.

Sending someone sexual emails or texts is written harassment. Visual is probably the hardest to spot because it can be very subjective. It includes wearing clothing with vulgar messages and displaying posters or pictures of a sexual nature. Verbal harassment is prevalent in schools, work, and everyday life. It's essential for victims and bystanders to address the behavior.

> *My male vice president, who I had previously rebuffed when he made an advance, suggested I needed to cover up my body because this wasn't a "T&A" appearance. I didn't know what that meant at the time and was appalled to learn it meant "tits and ass." At the time, I was wearing a well-tailored blue pinstripe skirt suit and rose silk camisole, which was certainly appropriate and professional. It was revolting and resulted in my reporting it to human resources. Although the CEO verbally reprimanded the vice president, most of the blowback fell on me, and I lost access to preferred work because he would not communicate with me.*
>
> **—Michele, Canada**

Physical

Physical harassment on the job might be harder to recognize because, at times, it's subtle. It includes the unwanted touching of a woman or her clothing and following or standing too close on purpose. Half of the women surveyed said men had sexually touched them without their permission. Sharing pornography or requiring sexual favors in exchange for a promotion or job security falls into this category. Sometimes sexual harassment in the workplace is masked by mild banter, comments accompanied by sexual gestures, or awkward statements that portray women negatively.

Harassment may start as microaggression, but when offensive comments are repeated or the behavior becomes physical, it escalates into the realm of harassment. As with verbal harassment, physical harassment may or may not fall within workplace harassment laws. Women may not report it because they are embarrassed, don't want to draw attention to themselves, or simply hope it will go away. They may also be concerned about retaliation. A study conducted by Speak Out Revolution reported that harassment based on sex was the most important driver behind unfair treatment at work, impacting 55 percent of women. Due to only a small percentage of women reporting workplace harassment, men often get away with it.

> *As a senior leader, I was charged with keeping my eyes open for up-and-coming leaders. I observed a young man who worked in the warehouse as a lead. He was very personable and hardworking. His smile was bright and genuine. He knew English, but he oversaw a group of women who only knew English as a second language. They were dependent on him. As the company's needs grew, I was asked about people who could step into supervisor roles. I mentioned the young man I had come to know through leadership mentoring. They told me, "He's no longer here." "What? What happened?" I was shocked. "The women he managed came to human resources. He was trying to extort sex from them, and he threatened to fire them."*
>
> **—Jed, United States**

Online

Online harassment has become an epidemic and affects 41 percent of women of all ages. The online harassment of women, sometimes called cybersexism, is gendered abuse targeted at women and girls. The purpose of the harassment includes wanting to embarrass, humiliate, scare, threaten, silence, extort, or encourage mob attacks. Online abuse involves a variety of tactics, ranging from sharing embarrassing content about a person to impersonation, doxing, stalking, electronic surveillance, nonconsensual use of photography, and violent threats.

Young women are more likely to experience sexual harassment

online. Plan International, a charity focused on equality for girls, surveyed 14,071 teenagers and young women aged 15–25 across 22 countries, including Australia, Canada, Brazil, Benin, Japan, Zambia, and the United States. Globally, 58 percent of the respondents reported experiencing online harassment.

The most common type of online harassment was abusive and insulting language, followed by deliberate embarrassment, body shaming, and threats of sexual violence. Those surveyed indicated that online harassment caused mental and emotional distress and fear for their physical safety due to threats. A disturbingly high number of girls worldwide are subject to harassment when they go online, in addition to being hassled on the street. There is no place where girls are safe and free from harassment.

Women in the public arena, including politics, experience severe online abuse regardless of age. A research team monitoring the social media mentions of thirteen prominent politicians in the United States, including Vice President Harris, Alexandria Ocasio-Cortez, and Ilhan Omar, found more than 336,000 instances of gendered and sexualized abuse posted by over 190,000 users. Those numbers represent just a small portion of the abuse women in public life deal with daily.

The harassment women experience online is intersectional. Women targeted because of their race, ethnicity, sexuality, or disability face abuse that intersects with sexism and report higher rates of emotional and psychological harm. The intent of abusive online sexist harassment is to silence women's voices. To push them off of social media platforms. When that happens, the harassers regain power and control, and the world loses women's contributions.

For a woman of my age, a baby boomer, sexism has been a part of my life since childhood. Beginning with my father, the rules for girls were different from those for boys. It was assumed, always, that my desires and ambitions were less critical than those of the men in my life. In graduate school, avoiding sexual advances from male professors was a natural part of student life. It was a long time before I learned to confront, rather than skirt, those advances. Second-wave feminism was a revelation to me, as I learned, at last, to break free from the oppression of assumed male superiority.

—Queen, United States

Bullying

Bullying is a pattern of repeatedly and deliberately harming and humiliating young girls who are more vulnerable than the bully. The term bullying is also used in organizations to describe the verbal harassment that employees experience. In *Antisexist*, bullying pertains to young girls as a form of harassment that starts at a very young age. It's often the first time a girl encounters sexist harassment.

Studies indicate that bullying peaks around ages 11 to 13 and decreases as children grow older. Girls are bullied more than boys. According to a survey conducted by YouthTruth, which collected feedback from 180,000 U.S. students in grades five through twelve, 30 percent of girls experience bullying. While cyberbullying does occur, most bullying happens in person, and the most common type is verbal, followed by social. Bullies can be boys or girls.

The primary reason girls indicated they were being bullied was their appearance. Bullying is microaggression being used by children at a young age to punish girls whose appearance doesn't fit the stereotype—stereotypes that come from experiences at home, school, and the media. In the case of bullying, sexism may intersect with other biases, including racism and ableism. Children often don't want to tell anyone about it because they think it will lead to more bullying. Girls who are bullied are impacted emotionally, academically, and mentally. Parents must educate their children about sexist microaggression and how it contributes to bullying. Schools need to create a safe environment for students.

> *My 12-year-old daughter wore a new sweater to school. She came home in tears. The boys started coming up to her at school and asking for hugs. At first, the hugs were quick, and then the boys began hugging her tighter. The boys made inappropriate comments about her breasts, and the girls started laughing. I think this was my daughter's first experience with sexual harassment and bullying. I talked to her about both topics, and I let her know that boys being mean to you doesn't mean they like you. I told her she deserved to be treated with respect, and I described respectful behaviors. It breaks my heart. She is so young.*
>
> —**Phoebe, Australia**

Street

Street harassment includes unwanted comments, gestures, or acts directed at women in a public space without their consent. Some 66 percent of women in the United States indicated they had been sexually harassed in public. Street harassment is typically done with the intent to frighten or dominate the targeted individual. It is once again about men establishing power and control over women.

When a man on the street comments on a woman's appearance, it may be done so quietly it's invisible to others. Usually, women who are targeted by street harassment ignore the behavior. Similar responses happen when women are harassed at work or online. When women are young, they are taught to ignore school bullies, so they do the same with the harassers they encounter as adults.

Women are also afraid that a response might escalate the situation and make the harasser more aggressive. Street harassment ends up making women feel violated or threatened. Women often modify their behavior by wearing different clothes or taking different paths. The responsibility to change should not belong to women, the victims, when the root cause is men. Street harassment is not about women's clothing or behaviors; it's about domination and power. The perpetrators are still dangerous regardless of what women do differently. Men and boys need to understand that not being a harasser is not enough. Engaging them in the solution is critical as it's men's responsibility to challenge each other's behavior.

The number of women experiencing street harassment is high worldwide. In a study conducted by UN Women about the experiences of women in the United Kingdom, 71 percent of women of all ages experienced some form of public sexual harassment. The number was 86 percent among 18-to-24-year-olds. The research found that women of color are disproportionately affected by street harassment. Women said they didn't report the harassment as they didn't think it would help or make a difference.

No form of street harassment should ever be considered a compliment, including catcalling, which involves demeaning and degrading sexualized comments. Several countries have taken steps to make street harassment illegal. France passed a law against verbal sexual harassment that allows law enforcement officers to sanction perpetrators on the spot instead of making victims wait for a trial later.

Frequently on social media, women will pose the question, "Women, if there were no men in the world for 24 hours, what would you do with that day?" The thousands of worldwide responses are primarily focused on doing things that men often take for granted. For those 24 hours, women would have the freedom to go out and not worry about being harassed by men. Women want that same freedom every day of their lives when men are present, but they don't have it. Here are a few examples of what women said they would do with those 24 hours.

I could go for an early morning walk and feel safe. I could walk to my car when it's dark without having my keys laced through my fingers for protection. I'd go through the entire day without being told to smile. I could sit on public transport without having a man crowd my space. I could go to a club and not have some random guy start groping me.

I wouldn't have to worry about being catcalled when I walked down the street. I'd go for a walk at night. I wouldn't be afraid to post something on social media that would give away my location. I could wear whatever I wanted out of the house without fear. I wouldn't have to downplay my accomplishments or intelligence.

I would go for a hike in the woods alone to enjoy nature and not worry about my safety. I'd tell my daughters to freely take a walk at night without their pepper spray. I'd let my girls walk home in the dark from a friend's home, and I wouldn't worry about them. I'd walk out to the nearby common at midnight to look at the moon. I'd go for a run at night.

I'd help abused women and children get to shelters. I would go to a park outside the city and lie down to watch the stars with my headphones on. I'd go to sleep with all my windows open. I'd take a midnight walk on the beach, lie down on the sand, and close my eyes, knowing I would be safe.

Flashing

Flashing is sexual harassment that happens when a man exposes his genitals to a woman, typically in public. Cyberflashing usually involves men sending women obscene pictures of genitals, dick pics via Airdrop, or other forms of technology. The victims of cyberflashing are not the subject of the photographs but they are the recipients, and they don't know the men that are flashing them. It's a growing problem for young women.

A study in the United Kingdom found that 32 percent of girls said they'd received an unwanted photo of a penis. Approximately 30 percent of the women surveyed in the United States had experienced unwanted genital flashing in a public place. Flashing in the street or via technology violates behavior that should never be normalized. Cyberflashing is just as traumatic as in-person flashing. Some governments have criminalized street flashing and cyberflashing.

Flashing of any type is threatening, as there is a high probability that flashers will commit other sex crimes. One study showed that 5–10 percent of perpetrators are caught for a more serious sexual offense in the five years following an offense for indecent exposure. Another study estimated that 80 percent of rapists began with noncontact sexual behaviors. There is nothing funny about indecent exposure. Flashers, like the police officer that murdered Sarah Everard, work up to committing more serious crimes. He had been reported for flashing women several times before Sarah's murder, yet there were no repercussions. Men who expose themselves aren't lonely and harmless; they are dangerous.

When I was 15, I walked past a man standing on a corner. Suddenly, he runs in front of me, and he is grinning. Then I notice he is holding his penis and rubbing it. I was shocked and frozen to the spot. I finally came to my senses and ran away. It scared me, and I never felt completely safe in public spaces after that. When my younger sister was 12, a man in a car harassed her by making comments about her body. She told me about it, and I had to say to her that it was all part of being a girl and that it probably wouldn't be the last time she would experience harassment by a strange man on the street. I felt awful telling her that it was normal and to find ways to deal with it.

—Emily, England

Challenge Sexism, Champion Women's Rights, and Create Equality

Following is a list of actions that men and women can take to stop sexist harassment and be antisexist. Review the list and add items to your Antisexist Action Plan.

Raise awareness about harassment by discussing it with others and bringing attention to harassing behaviors.

- Men need to talk with other men about sexism and harassment. Take a stand and speak up about sexism when you see it.
- Talk to your son and explain respectful behavior at school, work, online, and on the street. Explain sexism and bullying.
- Report harassment that you witness at work.
- Talk with friends or family members if you know they are involved in online harassment.
- Discuss harassment with friends or family members if you see them harassing a woman by catcalling, whistling, or making sexual comments.
- Step in and stop online harassment if you witness a woman being harassed.
- Men can join organizations for men that focus on changing harassing behavior and ending sexism.

Talk to your daughters about harassment. It's critical that they have knowledge about the abuse women experience.

- Explain sexism, respectful behavior, consent, and the types of harassment they could experience.
- Talk to them about bullying and explain it's not appropriate for boys or girls to bully others.
- Help them to understand how to handle various types of harassment.

When women experience harassment at work there are recommended steps to take in case legal action is required. Take the actions that feel most comfortable to you.

- Tell the person to stop.
- Document the behavior.
- Report the behavior to your manager.
- Report the behavior to human resources.
- You may want to consult with an attorney, as certain forms of workplace harassment are illegal in some countries.

Women experiencing online harassment should remember that the internet is available to everyone. No one has the right to push you off the online platform.

- Practice basic digital security.
- End the conversation and block the harasser.
- Document and take screenshots of inappropriate images and report them to the appropriate authorities.

Women experiencing street harassment should take actions to remove themselves from danger.

- Ignore the person. Don't engage with the harasser. Start talking to someone on your phone. Walk away.
- Go somewhere safe. If you are being followed, go into a local business and, if it feels safe, get help from a police officer or security guard.
- Report the harassment. Some forms of street harassment, depending on the country, are illegal.
- Take care of yourself and do what is best for you. Do whatever makes you feel safest. Trust your judgment.

If you are a bystander and witness a woman being harassed in public, when in doubt, assume you should help.

- Step in and offer support. Sometimes you can end the harassment by walking up to the woman and asking her questions about the time or directions.
- Check in with the woman being harassed and ask if she is all right.
- You can report the harassment you witnessed to law enforcement.

Encourage open conversations about harassment and allow others to share their experiences.

- Listen to someone's story without judgment.
- Never blame the victim. It's not the woman's fault because of how she looked or what she was wearing. No one is to blame but the harasser.
- Share your experiences of harassment with others. It can help raise awareness and eliminate the shame.

TEN

Feminism Is the Battle, Womanism Is the War

By Marri Champié

Putting a door on the female mouth has been an important project of patriarchal culture from antiquity to the present day. ... Greek thinkers convinced themselves that women belong to a different race than men.

—ANNE CARSON

I've learned that gender bias, bullying, and misogyny take a toll on the life of a warrior. It was Christmas 2019. I was recovering from foot surgery and had made my annual two dozen streusel apple pies to give to friends. I had a dozen to drop off at my favorite doctors. I drove around delivering pies, with a final delivery to my pain management doctor.

I didn't usually take advantage of the temporary handicap parking tag on my truck's rearview mirror, but there were no other open spaces. I parked to the left of the door, where both handicap spots were open. My big red diesel 1-ton truck barely fit into the handicap parking spot. I grabbed my four-legged old lady cane and the pie. I knew it would only take two minutes to deliver the pie to the desk.

Less than two minutes later I was walking out when a big guy pushed the door open to enter the office and blocked the door. He was almost as wide as the door, and I couldn't pass.

"I see you have a handicap parking tag, like I do," he said. "But your tires are parked over the line. You're taking up two spaces."

"I'm just leaving," I said. "I was only a minute. You're blocking the door."

The waiting room was crowded, and everyone glanced at us. He moved, and followed me to my truck.

"I had to park over there," he said, waving in the direction of a small truck about twenty feet further than where I was parked.

"You walked over here to tell me that? Are you going to keep yelling?"

"I'm not yelling."

"There are two open handicap spaces right there," I said, pointing to the spaces on the right of the door.

"You're taking up two spaces."

"After I move, you can go back to your truck and move it closer so you will be able to walk to the door." I don't remember if I let him hear my sarcasm.

He opened his mouth and closed it again. I wanted to smack him with my cane. I never react well when I'm confronted by a man who is a bully. He'd come into the doctor's office to start a fight with me or he wouldn't have followed me back out. He had already checked to see if I had a handicap sticker. There were other open handicap spots. He didn't need to come in to the office to correct me, but that's exactly what he attempted to do. He wanted to confront me and embarrass me in front of everyone. That's what bullies do. That's what men who are dismissive of women do.

From the time I was a small girl in the 1950s I pushed back against misogyny, gender bias, and bullying. I was expelled from second grade for three days because I knocked a boy's front tooth out. He got his tooth knocked out because he picked on the girls, lifted their skirts, and pulled their hair. One day, when he made a girl cry, I knocked him down. That's what I wanted to do to the huge man who confronted me in the doctor's office at Christmas. Anger over the incident possessed me for days afterwards. I couldn't think about anything else.

In the summer of 1988, I went on a fire assignment in a national park. I was thirty-eight years old and a stay-at-home mom living in a tiny mountain town in central Idaho. It was my first job away from home. I was hired to be a fire support driver working for a division of the fire program called Ground Support. Basically, I was Uber for fire. I came with a 1979 Ford F-250 truck with manual transmission and no power steering. I brought my tent and sleeping bag.

There were almost a hundred trucks and drivers on our fire alone, and only a handful of the drivers were women. In 1988, women were just beginning to gain a foothold in wildfire fighting occupations. There was a scattering of women on hand crews, more in the native crews than district crews, next to none in overhead positions, and zero women in Ground Support.

I stayed in the national park for eight weeks, cycling through four different overhead management teams. The Ground Support leader assigned me to drive a division supervisor when the second team, a Type One team, came on the fire. The equipment manager who worked in Ground Support didn't like it and objected, but the division supervisor insisted because my former passenger, the dozer boss, had told him I was the driver he wanted. After the first day I drove the division supervisor around, he requested me for his personal driver for the rest of his fourteen days. Again, the equipment manager objected, but was overruled.

We worked eighteen-hour days, driving every bulldozer trail and fire line on that fire, until my hands were cracked and bleeding. I had a nasty bruise on my elbow because my arm had slammed into the door when that old Ford with no power steering hit a hidden rock. We often got into fire camp late, and I would have to choose between eating dinner or taking a shower before both closed. The shower won, every time.

One night we got in just after dark. I barely noticed that all the other trucks were backed into their places in the paved campground parking lot. I tiredly parked the big truck in the single remaining space in the lot. My boss jumped out and headed to dinner. I climbed into the bed of the truck and was emptying and straightening the coolers. The equipment manager appeared beside my open tailgate.

"What the fuck are you doing?" he yelled.

"Getting ready for tomorrow," I replied.

"Why didn't you back in?" he yelled.

"Why should I?" I replied.

"Because I told everyone at our noon meeting to back in when parking," he continued to yell. Everyone in the campground stopped what they were doing to watch us.

"We were out on the fire," I said.

"That's no excuse. Turn this truck around," he yelled.

"Do I have to do it right now? I could barely get it in this spot." I was exhausted, my hands were bleeding, and I was about to not have dinner or a shower. The parking lot was cramped, so turning the truck around without power steering was going to be a real challenge.

"If you can't drive this truck, you don't belong on a fire. Women don't belong here anyway. Maybe you should go home, like the other gal (he used another name) did." He was still yelling.

"OK, give me a minute," I said. I wanted to finish in the back before I climbed out.

"Do it now," he yelled.

I was flustered, but I didn't want to lose my job. It was dark and I was tired. When I stepped to the tailgate and jumped off, the ledge of the sole of my leather Frye boot toe caught beneath the stainless trim strip on the tailgate, and I went headfirst off the back of the tailgate. I saved myself from cracking my head on the pavement by putting out both hands. I got to my feet, both hands and elbows bleeding.

"Hurry up," he yelled.

"Stop yelling at me!"

By this time the division supervisor I was driving had come back to the parking lot. While I turned the truck around, he and the Ground Support guy got into a heated argument. I parked the truck and slunk away.

The next day, my boss brought paperwork for me to file a complaint. I didn't want to. I told him I could handle it. He insisted that I do it "for all the other women out there who can't stand up for themselves," such as the other woman driver who had gone home in tears the day before. He was right, and so I filled out the paperwork. Then I was transferred from Ground Support to Command to work directly for the deputy incident commander. I have been actively fighting the battle for all women to never go home humiliated and in tears ever since that day. I'm a fighter, so I don't mind.

It's the all-consuming personal reaction I have to the patriarchy that is the bigger problem for me. Gender bias, bullying, and misogyny have existed in Western culture since the Greeks valued catamites over wives and Aristotle proclaimed the sound of women's voices created chaos and excluded women from the Academy. I have been obsessed with single-handedly righting that wrong from age five.

My defensive, overreactive response whenever I am confronted with gender bias has made my life uncomfortable. My thoughts are prone to a consuming anger that sabotages my writing and has spoiled many a family dinner or meditative walk. It's probably why I am alone instead of still happily married.

In the last decade I've realized there are women who are supportive of the patriarchy and against feminists, just like many men. Many unevolved women are blind to their misplaced subscription to patriarchal ideology and mentally unable to recognize the weighty role they play in perpetuating gender intolerance and prejudice. Other women intentionally take on the role of defender of Christian Right family values. Their stubborn disavowal of responsibility and loud disapproval of feminism has compounded my frustration at the slow change in equal rights. The misogyny here in America is rooted in puritanical prudery that wants to own the woman's reproductive value while at the same time censoring her naked breasts.

This too will change, I tell myself. One day women will have equal pay. One day women will control their own reproductive rights. One day soon, a person who treats a woman dismissively will be considered a pariah and be ostracized socially. One day America will have a woman for president. Until then, it doesn't. Until then I must realize I am not the only person on earth fighting this battle.

In order to put more time and emotional value into my own legacy of writing, and into accomplishments that my grandchildren might find worthy of remembering, I must find a way to walk away from confrontations that sidetrack my life. I must find a way to ignore the unevolved behavior of others so my own evolvement doesn't unravel into defensive reactions or all-consuming anger.

I've always been ready to jump into battle for what is right and just and fair. I must learn to be a warrior whose actions are deliberate, graceful, and calm, not reactive, unproductive, and unflattering. I want to be the woman I believe I am. These are my thoughts on how to be a graceful warrior while fighting the war on womanism.

- Create a tool to defuse negative responses. As a woman who believes herself to be confident and strong, I want to learn to walk away from moments of confrontation where there's no win, where the problem isn't mine, and where every response diminishes me. A friend suggested I think of my granddaughter when I'm triggered. Thinking about my granddaughter makes me smile. I now use the mantra "Think of Beryn" when I feel triggered. For someone else it might be to chant a song, recite lines of a poem, or think about their dog. Find a method to change your focus when faced with offense or insult. Remember, this too shall pass.

- Strive for peace. A wise man said, "As far as it depends on you, be peaceful with all men" (Romans 12:18). Although that advice was given to a different audience by a man whose misogyny is questionable, the advice is good. If you want to have peace in your life, don't start the war. But, if someone else starts a battle, you do not necessarily have to walk away. That depends on you. All people long for peace, but war is so much easier to achieve.
- Live to fight another day. It isn't your job to solve all the world's problems. Pick your battles and choose the battleground. For me, the best battleground is media and story, and my strongest weapon is my writing. It's definitely not an unexpected, impromptu, public moment where fight-or-flight emotion disengages the connection between articulate speaking and the brain. Perhaps you can't win. Not that day. Not yet. The gender war against women is unreasonable, old, and so deeply ingrained in social conditioning that you may sometimes feel you are wrong. You are not. Never give in. You are a woman. You are strong. All you really need to be powerful is to know that.
- Draw the long breath and walk it off. Go for a walk, every day if you can. It's all about the rhythm of step and breathing, and the seasons and weather around you. Once upon a time, people walked more. Poets created verses when walking, and troubadours created songs. Generals created battle plans when riding for many miles, listening to the beat of the army. Now, we move quickly from one place to another, without rhythm or breathing, without drawing in the world around us. We don't create; we allow noise to substitute for melody. Walk, breathe,

let the boundless energy of the connected cosmos unwind the knots inside you.

- Replace the word "hate" with another word. Hate is an obsessive, overarching emotion. The word is filled with power. My counselor halted a conversation where I had used "hate" to describe something by saying to me, "Hate is a strong word." I asked him what I should say instead. He shrugged. I realized after a year of thinking on this that it's not the word but the power of the word I needed to replace. Perhaps you must replace the word "hate" with "kindness." If you don't find another word for hate, find another way to think about and describe the world around you.

Biography

Dell Award–winning author Marri Champié has ridden horseback into the heart of the world—the Sawtooth Wilderness—countless times, and holds an MA in English. Nominated for the Pushcart Prize in poetry in 2015, her work has appeared in *Cicada*, *ROAR*, *The Tishman Review*, *Alcyone*, *Abyss & Apex*, and others. She received the Boise State University President's Writing Award for fiction and poetry in 2013, and an Oregon Poetry Association Award in 2018. Her novel, *Silverhorn*, was released by Kasva Press in 2018. She works as a wildfire support driver and lives on a small ranch overlooking the Idaho Prairie with her horses and Jack Russell terriers. Her website is WriteIdahoWriter.com.

ELEVEN

How to Be a Bitch with Style
Liyah Babayan

*When people call me names, I see that as a victory because I know they
don't have any argument on the merits.*

—WISDOM OF MY GRANDMOTHER, LUSYA TER-SIMONYAN

I am spoiled by the universe. I'm living my best life and working my
dream career. I make a living playing dress up. I dress women, and
occasionally men, to feel their absolute best in clothing capturing
their identity. For me, styling their personality in material designs
happens only on the surface level. What I actually do on a daily basis
is protect and promote the First Amendment.

Our individual freedom of expression is what we put on each day
when we dress. I am in the business of free speech through my art, my
fashion designs, and my personal styling. I cherish liberty—women's
liberty specifically. The length of a woman's skirt, the dip of her
neckline, the inches of her heels are all measures of a woman's safety
in society. Her authentic power begins and ends with the fashion
freedom accessible to her. Her courage to wear red lips, short hair, or

adorn herself in perfume.

Some women in the West take this privilege for granted. These are not safe accessories for millions of women and girls deprived of individual freedom worldwide. I love fashion not because I love fashion but because I love freedom. My lonely path to becoming a self-made entrepreneur, designer, and stylist was not paved with luck or equal opportunity. Imagine being a 22-year-old refugee with no assets, bad credit history, and an outrageous student loan, walking into a bank to apply for a loan for a sustainable fashion boutique. This at a time when going green was associated with liberal fringe ideology.

Not only did I know nothing about business, but worse, I was not bankable, a term I heard echoed out of the mouth of every lender I encountered. I believed in my dream. The bankers and investors believed I would fail. Recognizing the value of networking with established women in business associations, I reached out to make connections. The problem was there were no women who looked like me in these groups, and I felt like I didn't belong. I felt like I was being recruited to be the diversity token in the room and at their events.

The small-town clique network did not serve me or my business needs. I felt their judgment from the moment I walked into the room. A young woman of color who loved her body and wasn't afraid to express her sensual feminine energy. I was in the fashion business! I would describe my wardrobe as somewhere between Fran Drescher on *The Nanny* and Cher. I dressed like I belonged in New York, Los Angeles, or Paris, anywhere with appreciation for style. I was in a hyper-conservative, fashion-and-diversity-deprived town in Idaho.

I wore casual, hot pink lipstick, big hair, Arabic eye makeup, cropped tops, fitted dresses, skirts or leather pants. I almost never wore jeans, T-shirts, or sneakers. This is how I was raised. How I saw women dress in my Armenian community: bright colors, animal print, fitted tops, and beautiful heels. Unapologetic about their womanhood, glamour, and confidence. I had no concept of business or business casual. My outfits packaged my personality so accurately it felt like I was wearing a second layer of skin. I felt good about my personal style, although it took me a long time to fall in love with my body type and features.

Women can be sexist toward other women. It would be untrue if we placed the blame for sexism, harassment, and discrimination against women solely on men. I have been mistreated more often by women based on my appearance than by men. What is unspoken is that women can be very cruel to other women. This is a reality many successful women navigate and survive universally.

Another reality for women is being labeled a bitch when you speak up for yourself. You are not a bitch when you tolerate mistreatment and abuse, but when you align with your inner power and call it out, you are a bitch. Women are held to a double, triple, and quadruple standard when it comes to our appearance and communication style. The same characteristics in a man—assertiveness, boldness, and questioning the status quo—are qualities of a go-getter. Women with these exact same qualities are dubbed troublemakers, not cooperative, not ladylike, or just a bitch. As if we need permission to be movers and shakers, or have to apologize for taking charge of our destinies.

I expected my life in America to be challenged by a new language and culture. If it wasn't for my best friend doing homework for me, I wouldn't have graduated high school. In fact, I was illiterate until I attended university. I knew how to speak, but I struggled horribly to read, write, and spell in English. It caused a deep feeling of insecurity and humiliation. I expected my future was going to be very difficult no matter what direction I chose. Since childhood, I have experienced one form of discrimination after another, including religious discrimination, ethnic persecution and violence, discrimination for being a homeless refugee, for not speaking English, for being a foreigner, and for being a person of color. I became used to it.

It was the acceptance that was rare and took getting used to.

Being perceived and treated as a stereotype because of my background was not shocking to me. What was shocking to me was the hateful backlash for being an ambitious, goal-driven woman. I bought into the myth of equal opportunity and believed there was excitement for self-determination and achievement. What I discovered was an invisible barrier for women who desire to succeed, an even higher invisible barrier for women of color, and an extremely high barrier for ambitious refugee or immigrant women. No one teaches or prepares you for this in school or when you arrive in America. Realizing this hurt my heart.

Accepting this reality over the myth of equal opportunity changed my life. I understood that there would be no doors of opportunity opened for me, that I would have to build my own doors. Against all odds, and with zero capital, I decided to open my business in 2007. Because no lender would invest in my vision of a sustainable fashion boutique, I opened my doors with very little inventory.

I saw each woman who walked in as a micro-investor in my dream. I did not see anyone walking through my doors as a customer. I saw vision stakeholders, clients, and co-creators of Ooh La La! Boutique. Providing consignment as an option opened up a flow of inventory from every possible diverse trend and style closet. This unique selection in fashion, jewelry, and accessories set Ooh La La! apart from traditional retail.

In one year, we went from zero to 2,800 individual consignors, crashing our inventory software. Growth was challenging, even painful at times. Even more rewarding was seeing the space evolve into a multigenerational inclusive shopping experience for fashion lovers of every background. I never joined a women's business association, as I knew these organizations were designed to exclude women like me. The boutique organically built a community of like-minded people who were conscious about the impact of their shopping habits, the importance of minimizing waste, and circulating the benefits of consignment. Unlike bankers, they became spiritually, emotionally, and financially invested in supporting the vision of Ooh La La!

As my business became stable, I felt a craving to learn something new. A need to be challenged from a new angle. A shift in my passions happened after becoming a mother; the concern and excitement for my children's future opened my eyes to the status quo of society. I desired to champion and contribute to education, not just for my own children but for all the children in our community. Valuing the diversity and perspective someone from my background could bring to the decision-making process, I applied to serve on the school board of trustees. The interview was intimidating.

I knew I had no chance of being selected, especially because I was young, a stylist, and from a minority background. But I replaced the voice of doubt in my head with the voice of courage and prepared myself to demonstrate my leadership qualities during the interview. I refused to compromise my identity, honesty, integrity, or directness to please the board, or to package myself as someone else. I would rather be not selected for who I was than be selected for who I was not.

I passed the interview process and was selected. I was proud to be the first woman of color to serve. I was honored to represent diversity on an education board and give voice to the historically marginalized families in our community. About a month after being appointed to serve on the school board, I was called to meet with someone on the board. He confronted me about a complaint he received from someone working in the school district regarding my outfits and heels. I was not dressing according to our school code and used inappropriate language regarding our xenophobia about minorities in responses on my personal social media.

This was only days after I was attacked at the town hall and told to get the fuck out of this country. I confronted the individuals who attacked me and took a stand against the anti-refugee sentiment rising in the community on social media. Our entire community felt the rise of xenophobia. My car and business were vandalized.

I didn't know which to be offended by first, being scorned for my physical appearance or being censored for speaking up against racism. Without emotion or hesitation, I defended myself and the personal parameters of my life and liberty. I did what only a real bitch would do. I emailed the entire school board to quash any misunderstanding of what I would tolerate as a new trustee. I told them that I would not be censored or silenced when speaking up against racism and xenophobia, and as a school district we should all have the courage to do the same. I told them to not disrespect or belittle me again by asking me to dress according to a school dress code policy outlined for our students.

Serving the same community that gave my family a second chance at life as refugees felt like my gratitude duty. I enjoyed working with the teachers to make improvements in our district to support them in the classroom. Teachers were heroes, defenders of free thought, independence, freedom, and our democratic way of life. After serving on the school board, I decided to run for city council.

Yes, I was a young, self-made entrepreneur, lifestyle blogger, stylist, single mama of two, assertive, high-heel-wearing, ambitious, Armenian, refugee candidate for city council. Why not? My education background was in Political Science and International Relations, plus I was a small-business owner and was raising a family in our city. Naturally the quality of our life and the use of our tax money was a concern of mine.

I was just as qualified as anyone past or present who served as a council member. I just had more stacked against me. I will never forget the nasty emails and messages I received after filing my candidacy, even death threats. I doubt any of the other candidates were harassed because of their ethnic background or asked if they were Muslim or not. It didn't intimidate me, because I knew their ignorance had nothing to do with me. They would project their hate on someone else if it wasn't me. I felt sorry for them, that they had so much hate in their heart. I was afraid for my family; these were real threats. I thought about withdrawing my candidacy, but my family and friends encouraged me to not let the ignorance of other people distract me.

I decided to run a diversity-centered campaign and represent all the various marginalized members of our community who are underserved and underrepresented. This was a beautiful campaign, and it was centered in grace. Win or lose, there was a sense of responsibility to pave a path for the next candidate of color. There was a sense of duty to represent the voices of historically disenfranchised people.

I was told to know my place, meaning I was brought here as a refugee and that I was to do only what was designated for refugees to do. Public office was no place for a refugee. I received calls harassing me at work, calling me a refugee bitch and a fake American. I was slut shamed online for wearing high heels, fitted dresses, and skirts to publicly humiliate me as a woman. All while my children listened and my parents watched.

When people call me names, I see that as a victory because I know they don't have any argument on the merits. Refugee and immigrant women who want more than a life of servitude in this country are seen as troublemakers, ungrateful or overambitious. Being called a bitch was an affirmation that I was staying true to my dreams, goals, and desires in life. I embraced the word and gave it new meaning. B.I.T.C.H. To be a bitch is to Be In Total Control of Herself. Here are a few of my thoughts on how to be a B.I.T.C.H. and control your destiny. Be a bitch with style, and I'll be a bitch with you.

- Have an Olympian work ethic. A bitch knows she is going to make mistakes and builds a system of stability. She believes what people reveal to her about themselves. She never complains and never explains, because her friends won't need it and her enemies won't believe it.

- Spend every fiber of your being creating quality and expecting quality in return. A bitch knows there is only one thing you can control in life: your effort. She trusts her instincts, as they are messages from the soul.
- Find that place inside yourself where nothing is impossible. A bitch knows the difference between enjoying her youth and destroying her future.
- Know how and when to change. A bitch admits when she is wrong. She helps uplift another bitch without announcing it to the world. She never forgets who was with her from the start.
- Incorporate your emotional and spiritual goals into material and practical goals in order to round things out. A bitch doesn't ask for permission to dream, create, and live her best life.

Biography

After surviving the anti-Armenian ethnic killings in Baku, Azerbaijan, Liyah Babayan and her family were resettled in Idaho through the CSI Refugee Program. Liyah became an entrepreneur at age 22, served on the school board, and was the first refugee to run for city council in Idaho. Liyah was recognized as one of Idaho's Women of the Year in 2015 and 2020, received the ACLU's Civil Rights Service Award, and was featured in *The New York Times*. Her book *Liminal: A Refugee Memoir* was published in 2018. In 2019 Liyah was invited to present her book and testimony in Congress in support of recognizing the Armenian Genocide. Liyah is the founder of MAKEPEACE, a skin care line made from organic potatoes, and donates soap to displaced people for every product sold. In her free time Liyah spends time with her two children. You can connect with Liyah at www.liyahbabayan. com, or Ooh La La! Boutique, www.oohlala-shop.com.

TWELVE

Four Outcomes of Sexism: Violence

Statistically speaking, the most dangerous place for a woman is in her own home, not in the streets.

—Gloria Steinem

Hannah Clarke's husband ambushed her and their three children as Hannah prepared to take the children to school. He doused his wife and children with gasoline and set them on fire, killing them all. He then stabbed himself to death. Like many women, Hannah's tragic story isn't one of a few minutes of unbelievable terror and violence; it's a story of domestic violence and coercive control that played out over the years. Hannah's husband didn't beat her, so no one saw signs of physical abuse; he used other methods to control her. His methods of control included rape, stalking, verbal abuse, isolation, gaslighting, and technological surveillance. He controlled every aspect of her life and turned her home into a prison. It took years for Hannah and her family and friends to realize what was happening.

When Hannah finally realized her life was in danger, she and the children left her husband and moved in with her parents. She was unaware that a cluster of three risk factors in relationships—coercive control, violence, and a recent separation—increases women's risk of intimate partner homicide by 900 percent, according to the U.S. National Center for Injury Prevention and Control. Such a horrific crime shouldn't have led to victim blaming, but it did when an Australian detective said, "… is this an instance of a husband being driven too far by issues that he's suffered, by certain circumstances, into committing acts of this form?" It appears that women are to blame for everything.

Violence against women is defined as an act of violence that results in physical, sexual, or mental harm or suffering to women, including threats, coercion, or deprivation of liberty. Every day, 137 women worldwide are killed by a current or former partner or a family member. Women account for 82 percent of victims killed by their partner or ex-partner, according to a United Nations report on femicide. Eighty-seven thousand women and girls were murdered worldwide in 2017, and 50,000 of them were murdered by a current or former partner or a family member.

Violence against women, one of the four outcomes of sexism, is often based on sexist beliefs that men should be in control and have the power to dominate women and their behavior. The power differentials place women at risk for multiple forms of violence. Men who hold those sexist views are more inclined toward committing femicide.

Domestic violence, which describes women's experiences of violence in the home, can be misleading as it implies a focus on physical violence. Domestic violence is a pattern of behaviors used by one partner to maintain power and control over the other partner within an intimate relationship. The tools of control within domestic violence include isolation, stalking, emotional abuse, financial abuse, intimidation, threats, sexual abuse, and physical violence. Movies display domestic violence as volatile anger, thrown objects, black eyes, and broken bones. When those things aren't present in a relationship, it can be hard to recognize domestic violence. Domestic violence is a global problem that affects 35 percent of women worldwide.

At least 158 countries have passed laws on domestic violence. But even when laws exist, it doesn't mean they are consistently implemented or enforced. Women are often not believed, are victim blamed, and are denied police protection. Because of this, less than 40 percent of women who experienced violence sought help. Those who did seek help went to family and friends for support. Less than 10 percent of women who sought help went to the police.

Violence against women results in high costs to the countries, victims, and communities involved. Costs are both direct and indirect, and tangible and intangible. In 2021, the cost of violence against women in the European Union was estimated at around 289 billion euros a year. Based on five million domestic violence cases per year, the cost to the United States is about 460 billion dollars a year. Domestic violence causes severe physical, mental, sexual, and reproductive health problems for women, and their children suffer as well.

FOUR OUTCOMES OF SEXISM	
Microaggression	**Discrimination**
Sexist Language	Education
Stereotypes	Employment
Objectification	Wage Gap
Shaming	Career
Mansplaining	Healthcare
Invalidation	Sexual
Harassment	**Violence**
Verbal	Physical
Physical	Sexual
Online	Emotional
Bullying	Economic
Street	Coercive Control
Flashing	Femicide

Six Types of Violence

The six types of violence toward women and girls that frequently occur are physical, sexual, emotional, economic, coercive control, and femicide. They are all methods of maintaining power and control primarily used by men against women. Physical violence involves hurting or trying to hurt women and may include property damage. Sexual violence includes forcing women to participate in a sex act without consent. Undermining women's sense of self-worth through constant criticism is emotional violence.

Economic violence makes women financially dependent by maintaining total control of financial resources. Coercive control is a type of psychological violence designed to make women dependent by isolating them from support, exploiting them, denying their independence, and monitoring daily behavior. Femicide refers to the intentional murder of women because they are women and can be defined broadly to include any killings of women and girls.

Physical

Francine Hughes suffered physical abuse by her husband for 13 years. The beatings began on their honeymoon when Francine was 16 years old. Francine did not press charges against her husband as she was afraid for her life. Professionals offered little help, suggesting assertiveness training and tranquilizers. They continued to live together with their four children even after they divorced. On March 9, 1977, police responded to her report of a domestic dispute. Her husband warned her that "it was all over" for her because she called the police. When the police left, she was beaten and raped by her husband for hours. When he fell asleep, she picked up a gas can, went into the bedroom, and set the bed and her husband on fire. She then gathered up her children, went to the police station, and turned herself in.

She was found not guilty of murder at the trial because of temporary insanity. Her story was dramatized in the 1984 television movie,

The Burning Bed. The case, book, and television movie were credited with altering public perceptions of domestic violence, redefining it as a crime rather than a private affair. The concept of battered woman syndrome, a form of post-traumatic stress disorder, was created. It also prompted the establishment of domestic violence shelters across the United States. Until 1984 domestic abuse or wife-beating was kept hidden behind closed doors.

Physical violence includes hitting, kicking, burning, grabbing, pinching, shoving, slapping, hair-pulling, and biting. Other examples of physical violence are withholding physical needs such as sleep or food, locking the victim out of the house, denying medical help, and forcing alcohol or drug use. It can include property damage. Globally, one in three women have been subjected to either physical or sexual violence in their lifetime, either by an intimate partner or non-partner. Over a quarter of women aged 15–49 in a relationship have been subjected to intimate partner violence.

Sexual

Sexual violence is any sexual act committed against a woman's will, either when she does not give consent or when she cannot give consent because she is a child, has a mental disability, or is severely intoxicated or unconscious due to alcohol or drugs. Sexual violence includes rape, trafficking, female genital mutilation, and child marriage. Rape is any nonconsensual vaginal, anal, or oral penetration of another person with any body part or object.

On the evening of January 17, 2015, Chanel Miller went to a fraternity party with her sister. Later that night, two graduate students found her lying unconscious on the ground behind a dumpster, being sexually assaulted by a male student. The male student tried to run but was held down by the two graduate students until the police arrived. In the early hours of the morning, Chanel was at the hospital having her vagina and anus swabbed by police doctors. The male student was arrested and indicted on five felony sexual assault charges, to which he pleaded not guilty.

What happened next was a textbook example of the double standards that often exist in sexual assault cases. Chanel's assailant was a champion swimmer from an affluent family who was considered to have potential, an upstanding young man who surely would never commit assault. Chanel was referred to as the stereotypical drunk girl at a fraternity party and victim blamed. It was her credibility that was questioned and on trial, not his.

There were many sexist biases at work, including the assumption that the consumption of alcohol turns a woman into a slut, but excuses a man for sexual assault. Chanel's assailant was convicted of three charges and sentenced to six months' imprisonment. The public was outraged by the sentence's leniency and the judge's statement that the reason he chose to issue such a light sentence is that prison would have had a severe impact on the assailant. The judge was recalled two years later.

Chanel was humiliated by the light sentence. She read a 12-page victim impact statement in court that was published anonymously online and went viral. She received tremendous support from millions of people around the world. What is so horrific is that by the standards of most women who are raped or sexually assaulted, Chanel's experience was good, comparatively speaking. According to the Justice Department, fewer than one percent of sexual assaults in the United States result in felony convictions. This case is a story about sexual consent and the importance of understanding and honoring a woman's ability to give consent. If a woman is unconscious, she can't give consent, and when a woman says "no," it means "no."

Pornography is one cause of the normalization of violence in sex that can contribute to an expectation of nonconsensual sex. Rough sex, which includes nonconsensual behaviors including choking and rape, can escalate to other types of violence against women. Billie Eilish, at twenty years old, discussed the impact that viewing pornography online had on her. She said she was about eleven when she first saw pornography and that it gave her nightmares. Viewing pornography changed her expectation of what sex should be. She indicated that the first few times she had sex, she wasn't saying no to things that weren't good. She now believes that pornography is a disgrace.

The number of children exposed to pornography is significant. One study found that 51 percent of children ages 11 to 13 had seen pornography online. Pornography is easy to access and likely to be seen by those below age restrictions. Girls feel pressured to accept the sexual violence seen in porn or be considered uptight. The recommendation is that parents talk early and often to their children about pornography, sexual harassment, and consent. Educators need to address the impact of pornography as a component of sexual education. The detrimental effect of pornography on physical and sexual violence against women is significant.

Another sexual abuse trend is intimate image abuse, which includes posting revenge porn, circulating women's images and details, and passing on private nudes. Multiple platforms exist for that very purpose, to provide men a place to post revenge porn or nude photos. There is a collector culture where men post requests for specific images. They post, collate, and trade intimate images of women. These men are typically boyfriends, ex-boyfriends, husbands, and ex-husbands of the women whose photos are posted. Whether or not these women permitted the pictures or videos to be taken is irrelevant; they did not allow them to be shared on a public site. There should be no victim blaming.

One study that included Australia, New Zealand, and the United Kingdom indicated that one in five men had been perpetrators of intimate image abuse. These men and boys posting aren't the occasional perverts; they are everyman. While some revenge porn is made public and the women who are targets are aware, much of the sharing of intimate images is kept secret. Women allowing intimate photos or videos to be taken are putting themselves at risk. The viewers of these images don't consider women to be human beings. All aspects of intimate image abuse dehumanize women, and the impact is destructive. In some countries, posting such images without permission is illegal. However, it can be tough to get such cases prosecuted.

Sex trafficking is another type of sexual violence. Trafficking is the acquisition and exploitation of women through force, fraud, coercion, or deception. Millions of women and girls worldwide get trafficked and sexually exploited. In 2018, 92 percent of the detected victims of trafficking for sexual exploitation were women. The convictions of Jeffrey Epstein and Ghislaine Maxwell for sex trafficking young girls over a ten year timeframe showed that sex trafficking could happen anywhere and to anyone. The case brought much-needed attention to the crime of sex trafficking. Victims tend to be young girls, and they may meet their trafficker online. It's easier to manipulate girls, and the average age of entry into sex trafficking is between 11 and 14. Trafficking doesn't only involve the poor or immigrants; the citizens of a country and the wealthy are also targeted.

Female genital mutilation is a form of sexual violence that women and girls experience. It includes procedures that intentionally cause injury to the female genital organs for nonmedical reasons. Female genital mutilation is a social norm, typically driven by sexist beliefs about sexual expression. It's often considered necessary to prepare girls for adulthood and marriage. Two hundred million women and girls worldwide have experienced female genital mutilation.

Child marriage, another form of violence against women, is any marriage where one or both spouses are below the age of 18. Girls are more likely to be child brides. Once married, girls frequently drop out of school and experience domestic violence. Each year, 15 million girls worldwide are married before the age of 18.

Emotional

Emotional violence is a way to control a woman by using emotions to undermine her sense of self-worth through constant criticism. It can involve demeaning her abilities, name-calling, or other verbal abuse. A consistent pattern of abusive language and bullying behavior wears down a woman's sense of self-esteem and undermines her mental health.

Emotional violence can be one of the most challenging forms of abuse to recognize. It's often subtle and manipulative. The signs of physical abuse might be noticeable to friends and family, but the effects of emotional abuse are harder to see and prove. Emotional damage can often take longer to heal. Emotional abuse not only takes place in personal relationships, but it can also happen on the job. Women can be emotionally abused by their managers or other employees.

> *I endured a brief relationship with a man from another culture who initially seemed intelligent and charming. He "love bombed" me, drawing on my vulnerabilities, which he later used against me in frightening episodes in which I'd fear for my life. He was retroactively jealous of my past relationships, quickly isolated me, and wouldn't listen to the word no. He locked me in the house, and I was subjected to physical and sexual abuse, coercion, and gaslighting. He threatened to kill himself whenever I escaped. He used his refugee status to guilt me into returning. I was exhausted, and he wore me down. I left and returned three times before I contacted his ex-girlfriends, who told me they'd suffered similarly and that he'd been stalking them for years. The solidarity between me and his ex-girlfriends was extraordinary and not something he counted on. His narrow sexist view underestimated women and their innate care for one another. Though our contact*

ended, he continued to stalk me. I had to change my number three times and notify the police.

—**Alessia, Italy**

Economic

Economic violence involves making women financially dependent by maintaining total control over financial resources, withholding access to money, or forbidding attendance at school or employment. Because abuse is about power and control, an abuser will often use finances to maintain that control. It can involve controlling household budgets and not letting women access their bank accounts or spend money.

Economic violence can also include opening credit cards and running up debts in women's names or simply not letting them have a job. This type of abuse is often the main reason why women cannot leave an abusive relationship. Women end up with credit problems that affect their ability to get an apartment, job, car loan, and any number of other things necessary for independence.

Coercive Control

Coercive control is a type of psychological violence designed to make women dependent by isolating them from support, exploiting them, denying their independence, and monitoring their daily behavior. It's a strategy of psychological abuse consisting of abusive behaviors, but often legal. Behaviors that are normal within relationships become tools to instill fear and compliance. These behaviors may escalate slowly. For example, it's normal to occasionally check in with a partner via text or phone in a healthy relationship. Coercive control would involve check-ins several times a day, every day. Because these behaviors escalate slowly, it feels normal.

Coercive control often involves making women doubt their sanity. Women will depend on their abusers more and more as they trust their own judgment less and less. Coercive control can include isolation from friends and family, monitoring activity, stalking, denying freedom, gaslighting, making jealous accusations, regulating sexual activity, and threatening children or pets. Coercive control wears away at women's mental health and well-being. Women often don't tell anyone about what they are experiencing for fear of not being believed.

It's known that women who experience coercive control have severe limits placed on their human rights, including freedom of movement and independence. It's now recognized that coercive control is far more harmful than physical violence and has a long-lasting impact on women's sense of well-being. Coercive control is being taken seriously because it predicts physical violence. Men who have killed their female partners have usually dominated them first, often without physical violence. For those reasons, coercive control has been criminalized in a few countries, such as England, Wales, Ireland, France, Scotland, and Canada (Ontario). In the United States, Connecticut, California, and Hawaii have coercive control laws.

Femicide

Hannah Clarke. Vanessa Guillén. Oluwatoyin Salau. Gabby Petito. Sarah Everard. Sabina Nessa. Say their names. Say the names of any women you know who were murdered because they were women. In 2017, 87,000 women and girls worldwide were intentionally killed, with gender being the main reason. Intimate partners or ex-partners murdered fifty thousand. One hundred thirty-seven women worldwide are murdered every day by a current or former partner or family member.

Femicide is the killing of women and girls primarily because of their gender. They are murdered by misogynists, men who have a hatred for women, men who don't value women. Often, they are murdered by men that are their husbands, boyfriends, ex-husbands, fathers, brothers, sons, or other family members. Sometimes they are murdered by men they have never met, simply because they are women. Femicide is the most extreme form of violence against women.

The number of femicides is increasing worldwide. Some have described it as a femicide epidemic. Six women are killed every hour by men around the world, by men who are partners or family members. In the United States, in 2019, 1,795 women and girls were victims of femicide. That's an average of five U.S. women killed every day for being women. Men murder women of color at a rate two times higher than white women in the United States. A woman is killed by a man every three days in the United Kingdom.

Femicide occurs most often in Latin America, Africa, and Asia. In most countries, femicide is treated the same as any other homicide in criminal law. However, a few countries have specific laws about femicide. In the United States, the Violence Against Women Act was one such law, but it has expired and needs to be reauthorized by Congress to provide women with more protection.

Women are at the greatest risk of being murdered when attempting to leave an abusive relationship, as leaving is the greatest threat to the abuser's power and control. Another type of femicide that threatens power and control is honor killings, committed when a female is believed to have disgraced her family. The killing is thought to restore the family's honor.

Worldwide, more men are murdered than women. So why focus on femicide? Violence against women is unique, and it happens to perpetuate and maintain gender inequalities. Men are usually murdered by other men, often in gang-related violence or random crime that has nothing to do with intimate relationships. In contrast, women are frequently murdered by men they know because they are women.

Murder is a man's final attempt to gain power and control over a woman. Even when a stranger murders a woman, it often involves gender-related power and control, including rape. Femicides won't be reduced by telling women to stay home at night, carry mace or whistles, or other suggestions on how to behave so men won't murder them.

Femicides will only be reduced by eliminating beliefs and behaviors related to systemic sexism, misogyny, patriarchal ideology, and other systems supporting men's need for power and control over women and gender inequality.

Jennifer's Story

Go back to Chapter 1 and look at your pre-test, where you identified all the examples of sexism in Jennifer's story. Then look at the examples of sexism underlined below in Jennifer's story, each marked with one of the four outcomes of sexism that it aligns with: Microaggression (M), Discrimination (D), Harassment (H), and Violence (V).

Jennifer left the world the same way she entered it, helpless. Never fully understanding the role that sexism played in her life and death. She was caught in a trap for most of her brief life. A trap that many women and girls stumble into, unaware and often without the tools and resources needed to escape.

When she was born, her parents welcomed her into their lives with open arms, thrilled to add a little girl to their growing family. Jennifer's two older brothers were excited to have a sister. She was sent home wrapped in a pink blanket (M) with a wardrobe of pink onesies that said Princess, Daddy's Girl, and Little Cutie (M). As a young child, she played with her dolls and tea set that were gifts from her parents (M). When she attempted to play with her brothers' trucks, she was told those were toys for boys, not girls (M). She watched movies and read books about princesses saved by princes (M). She excelled in most subjects in school but found it hard to convey her knowledge. Her attempts to answer the teachers' questions were ignored as the boys were called on first (D). The teachers often complimented her for being quiet and well behaved, as girls should be (M).

As a teenager, Jennifer attended church each Sunday with her family. She learned that a woman's role was to support her husband (M). When her mother went back to work part-time, Jennifer was expected to clean the house and fix dinner for her brothers and father (M). She continued to excel in school and developed an interest in math and science. She talked with her school counselor about her interest in taking college preparatory courses in science. She was told that science wasn't a good career path for a girl (D). When she asked to join the science club, teachers told her to join a club more appropriate for girls (D).

At 16, she got a job waitressing in a local restaurant. One night she worked late at the restaurant. After everyone else had left, the manager asked to speak to her in the office. He asked her how things were going as he rubbed her arms and shoulders (H). He complimented her work. From then on, he scheduled her to work late at the restaurant at least once a week. The manager often invited her into his office when she worked late, and the rubbing and touching continued (H). Then one night, he pushed himself against her (H). He rubbed his crotch against her (V) while telling her how beautiful she was. She didn't know what to do. She was ashamed and embarrassed. The manager threatened to tell everyone she came on to him if she didn't keep quiet (H). She told no one what happened and asked not to work late shifts because of her school schedule.

When Jennifer was 17, she met Matt at a friend's house. Matt was 27 and had recently moved back to town. The connection was instantaneous, and the relationship progressed quickly. Soon Jennifer was only spending time with Matt, and her other friendships slipped away (V). Matt told her he didn't want to share her with anyone when she suggested spending time with her girlfriends (V). Jennifer felt flattered. Within a matter of months, she was pregnant. Matt proposed and urged a quick wedding at the city hall (V). Jennifer told her parents, who had never met Matt. They were concerned and angry but agreed to the marriage. Shortly after her high school graduation, Matt and Jennifer were married. Once married, he asked her to quit her job to stay home with the baby (V).

After the birth of their son, Jennifer quickly became pregnant again. Jennifer took care of her children during the day and Matt at night after their daughter was born. She rarely saw her parents and had lost contact with her friends (V). She relied on Matt for money and had no car or credit cards of her own (V). Matt began stopping by the bar after work with his friends. When he got home, he was often angry at Jennifer and criticized her cooking or housekeeping (V). The criticism became frequent, along with yelling and swearing (V). Then one night, he slammed her against the wall and slapped her hard (V). He apologized and told her how much he loved her the following day (V). But the criticism, yelling, and hitting continued, along with the apologies (V). Often the abuse happened in front of the children (V).

Jennifer felt isolated and alone (V). One day, after a particularly violent evening with Matt (V), she visited her mother with the children. She hadn't seen her parents in months. Jennifer's mother was shocked when she saw Jennifer's face and a black eye (V). She convinced Jennifer to go to the police station to file a complaint. They left the children with Jennifer's dad and drove to the police station. The police asked Jennifer if she was sure she wanted to file a complaint against her husband (M). They asked her why she hadn't reported any of this abuse previously (M). She was asked why she hadn't gone to the hospital (M). While Jennifer was being questioned, her father called, telling her that Matt had come to the house to pick up the children. Jennifer didn't know where he and the children were (V). She was afraid he might hurt them (V).

Jennifer finished filing the complaint. She told the police that her husband had her children and she had to find them. She told her mother she had to go home and wait for Matt. Late that night, Matt came home with the children. He knew Jennifer had gone to the police station. He apologized once again and told her he loved her (V). The next day Jennifer went to the police station and redacted her statement (V). <u>She said it all had been a misunderstanding, and</u> <u>everything was fine</u> (V). Then she went home.

Matt returned home that evening after drinks at the bar. <u>He walked</u> <u>into the house and shot and killed Jennifer and their two children</u> (V). He <u>then turned the gun on himself</u> (V). Jennifer's parents found them dead the next day. Jennifer was 22 years old; her two children were three and four. Jennifer died helpless. Nothing had prepared her to understand how to escape coercive control and domestic violence by a man she loved.

Challenge Sexism, Champion Women's Rights, and Create Equality

Following is a list of actions that men and women can take to stop violence against women and girls and be antisexist. Review the list and add activities to your Antisexist Action Plan.

Mike Cameron's girlfriend, Colleen Sillito, was murdered by her common-law partner. Her murder changed his life, and he formed a nonprofit, Ignore No More, that raises awareness about domestic violence. His suggestions to men on how to stop the abuse of women focus on managing sexist beliefs and attitudes, along with men exploring their emotions to cope with them healthily.

- Become an ally to women to effect change.
- Talk to your sons about sexism and what it means to be respectful.
- Talk to your friends about sexism and equality.
- Challenge your attitudes and beliefs about women that may have been instilled in you from childhood.
- Call out your buddies when they treat or talk about women as less than. Stop the locker-room talk.
- Allow your sons to feel and express their emotions.

- Allow the men in your life the space to safely explore their emotions without fear of being ridiculed.
- Challenge those that mock or ridicule men for expressing emotion.
- If you are committing any acts of violence toward women, or want to, seek professional help.

Talk to your daughters and other family members or friends who need to learn more about domestic abuse.

- Talk to them about what respect and consent look like and their expectations.
- Review the different types of violence they might encounter in relationships because they are women. Explain that not all abuse is physical.
- Let them know that you support them if help is ever needed.
- Discuss victim blaming and the fact that the abused woman, or murdered woman, is not responsible for the abuse. The abuser needs to be held accountable.

It can be genuinely frightening if you are a woman attempting to leave an abusive relationship. Here are some suggested steps to take once you have decided to leave. Don't face the decision alone.

- Map out your plan. List the safe places you can go to, along with the people who will provide you with support and protection against your abuser.
- Keep evidence of abuse. The evidence may include pictures of physical abuse, text messages, and threatening emails. Keep the proof well hidden.

- Discreetly reach out to local women's centers that provide support for victims of domestic abuse and can offer input to your escape plan. They often provide guidance for life after you have left your abuser.
- Call a domestic abuse helpline. These hotlines will offer anonymous help to domestic violence victims.

If you see any signs that your friend or loved one is being abused, offer to listen to her concerns and provide support. It can take an average of seven attempts to leave before an abused woman leaves her abuser for good. Patience will be required. Look for these signs of abuse.

- Obvious or hidden physical abuse, including cuts or bruises.
- Behaving apprehensively in the presence of her partner.
- Routinely making excuses for her partner's controlling or demeaning behavior in public.
- Having limited control over finances.
- Meeting less often with friends and family members.
- Demonstrating concern or fear about saying the wrong thing to her partner, contradicting her partner, or being unable to refuse sex.

THIRTEEN

The Abuser Disguised as a Knight in Shining Armor

By Elizabeth St. John

You save yourself or you remain unsaved.

—ALICE SEBOLD

Every once in a while, in the middle of an ordinary life, love gives you a fairy tale. Mine began in my late twenties when I met my future husband. He was my prince. He was smart, funny, kind, good-looking, successful, and the kind of man everyone immediately liked. In our eighteen years together, we had a good marriage, made many friends, enjoyed career success, raised two children, and traveled to amazing places. We lived a charmed life.

One beautiful October night we spent the evening at dinner with friends listening to live music. Back home, only hours later, my husband dropped dead in my arms of a heart attack. He was 47 years old. Our children were preteens, and they'd just lost their father. We were supposed to grow old together. This was not supposed to be my life. My world crashed down on me and my fairy tale was over in the blink of an eye.

After that fateful day, whenever I climbed into our bed, I relived the nightmare of watching my husband slip away and how I tried frantically to save him, but I couldn't. Each morning when I awoke, it was like the movie *Groundhog Day*. I'd remember that my husband was gone forever.

I was a young widow and my kids had no father. Same nightmare, different day. Those first months after my husband died were a blur of nonstop crying and asking *why*. In spite of my plight, I had to keep it together. People were depending on me, including my children and my business associates. I pressed forward, going through the motions. Looking back on those early months, I only survived by the grace of God, the support of my family and friends, and, honestly, medication. And I did meet a man, one I thought could be my knight in shining armor sent to protect me from my sorrow.

One night I forced myself to go to a friend's house for a small gathering. I remember feeling awkward being there when I was so sad. A man approached me, I'll call him Phil, who gave me his condolences. He seemed happy, which felt comforting. How refreshing it was to see someone smiling at me instead of mirroring the pain they saw in my face. Looking back, it seems creepy—fake charm unwarranted for a somber situation. As the song says, I can see clearly now the rain is gone. I was the perfect prey for a manipulative narcissist.

Before long, Phil and I started talking for hours by phone. He was sympathetic to my situation and so witty, like my late husband. One night, I remember my daughter knocking on my bedroom door as she thought I was crying, as I often did. But on this night, I was actually laughing with Phil. Joy certainly felt like the antithesis of grief. I hadn't planned on it, but we started dating.

After only four months, Phil told me he had fallen in love with me. I knew this was too fast, which scared me. I reminded him that I'd recently lost my husband and asked him to slow down. Phil pushed me to live with him, and though I was already under his charming spell, I had the wherewithal to say "No." So, he moved nearby instead. Then he showered me with romantic gestures and amazing vacations. He put me on a pedestal, and his grand gestures matched the intensity of my emotions.

Later I learned that he was love bombing me, which is a manipulation technique that narcissists use to win over their victims. I was naïve at the time, enjoying the feel-good distraction from the unbearable pain of losing my husband. Phil and I had great mental and physical chemistry. After making love, he would present my favorite treat, raspberry chocolate, which was conveniently located in his nightstand drawer. At the time, it seemed sweet. I mean, what woman doesn't like chocolate? But soon I came to know all too well his subtle system of rewards and punishment to train me to behave exactly as he wanted.

Early in our love affair, Phil and I had our first big fight. He thought I was flirting with another man, but I wasn't. His control and jealousy were surfacing. Most of the time, I felt adored by this man. When it was good, it was great. When it was bad, it was very *bad*. Phil was highly sensitive to perceived slights and was often angry with me. To punish me, he would deny me any communication and block my phone number for several days so we couldn't resolve things. For a woman who likes to talk things out, this was torture.

His silent punishment made me feel abandoned, which just intensified my feelings from losing my husband. It was a terrifying and horrible feeling. My intuition told me his silence wasn't healthy, but I needed to win back his love to feel safe again. I second-guessed myself, "Maybe I was married so long that I don't know how to act when dating again?" And, "He's just sensitive, and I should double my efforts to prove my love."

He seemed so confident most of the time, but then out of the blue he'd ask me, "Why are you with me? Isn't your type more like so-and-so?" Insert any manly man's name. We were already deep in the relationship, so these questions surprised me. He needed constant proof of my love. A narcissist's mask will sometimes fall off and you'll see their true self, which is insecure and filled with self-loathing. My mom told me once, "When someone tells you who they are, believe them."

I didn't listen to my intuition, despite warning signs. Once Phil told me he hired a service to scrub anything from the internet that had his name listed. Another time I was with him when he was denied purchasing a gun for target practice for our upcoming mountain vacation. I later found out his background check failed. His ex-wife had filed a domestic violence complaint and she had a restraining order against him.

The red flags were there, but I was caught in his web and it was sticky. I really thought I could rescue him and, at the same time, change him with my love. Because sometimes it's the princess who kills the dragons and saves the prince, right? A myth women often believe. We can't rid a man of his demons or change his behavior. As a confident, intelligent, middle-aged woman, you'd think I would have been wise enough to know better. But instead, I became more codependent on him and addicted to the highs and lows. A cycle of joy and adoration followed by abandonment and shame.

The people closest to me saw my path of destruction. In fact, one of my closest friends ended our friendship, in an email no less. My father tried to give me perspective. "It's like you're living with an alcoholic. Six days are great, then the seventh day ruins it!" My daughter once told me to choose between her and Phil. I chose him. My angry son left home and stayed elsewhere much of the time. I hardly noticed during my delusion.

Phil's abuse worsened. He could only go for a few months before blowing up, blaming me for not being perfect and calling me names. I remember being on vacation with another couple, and after a strenuous hike, we ate some appetizers I made. I polled them to see if I should make dinner, to which they all said no. Phil later yelled at me, saying I was both rude and lazy for not cooking dinner. Narcissists worry a lot about what others think of them.

I was loyal to Phil and didn't understand his distrusting nature. Once I was selling my jet skis and Phil insisted he go to the meeting with me since I was meeting a man. I assumed it was for safety. During that meeting, Phil tried to kiss me. Feeling embarrassed in front of the potential buyer, I pulled back. Afterwards, Phil was furious with me for not kissing him, yelled at me, and sped off in his car. Then he blocked my phone number again. In his eyes, this was just one more time I failed to prove my love. Therefore, punishment.

Phil also attempted to brainwash me to control me. During those afterglow moments in bed, he would often say the same thing, "Aren't you glad you're not lying on the chest of a hairy man right now? Wouldn't that be gross?" He was smooth-chested and didn't see himself as very masculine. He really wanted to convince me that I didn't need a masculine man.

The most glaring case of brainwashing came about after a night in a hot tub when I told him that my daughter was doing well in her acting classes and a Los Angeles agent saw her perform and was impressed. I mused out loud, "I wonder if we ever moved to California, if she might have a shot at an acting career? Curious, would you ever consider such a move with your job?" He immediately got upset that I would ever consider moving based on a child's dream.

Weeks later, he brought it up again at dinner out, but calmly this time. He said, "That comment you made about moving to Los Angeles with your daughter was irresponsible and shows you're a pathetic parent." I was shocked he called me a pathetic parent. Then he said it again, casually. Then again in a different sentence in a low, calm voice. Then again, stated differently. This SOB knew I was nervous about being a solo parent, and he was using it against me.

In disbelief, I left the table to visit the restroom. This time, it only took moments for the light switch to flip on. I walked back to our table and demanded we leave. In the car, he said it one more time as he shook his head in disgust, "You're a pathetic parent." I lost it and I said, "Get the fuck out of my car and the fuck out of my life!" I left him in the parking lot and drove home. His hold over me was finally broken. It turned out that my knight in shining armor was an abuser.

Free of Phil at last, I began the hard, emotional work of healing from my losses. I began the process of healing from this unhealthy relationship and its effect on my life. I lost friends, damaged my relationship with my children, and nearly lost my soul. Finally, over the many years that followed, I've found peace and come to terms with the loss of my husband. I still miss him. As they say, "Widows don't move on, they move forward."

Life is full of lessons. I've always believed that pain, if not shared, is wasted. I learned later that I had been abused emotionally by a narcissist. As a woman in a vulnerable emotional state, I was an easy target, as are many women. Emotional abuse is any kind of abuse that is emotional rather than physical in nature. It can include verbal abuse, constant criticism, and coercive control tactics such as intimidation, manipulation, and refusal to ever be pleased. Below are a few suggestions that may help you to recognize and prevent emotional abuse.

- Don't buy the myth that men will save you and make you feel safe. Not all men are good or emotionally healthy, and none can make you whole. Only *you* make you feel whole. When you feel low, ask for support from those close to you or from a professional. Learn self-love. Seek to gain peace and understanding through reflection, meditation, prayer, nature walks, music, and any inspirational activity which fills you up.
- Don't hurry love. If a relationship is authentic and real, you won't feel pressured to move fast. I learned the hard way that

if someone confesses their undying love for you and wants to lock you down quickly in a relationship, they either do not know their own mind and heart or they are controlling. Real love waits. A healthy mate doesn't require you to constantly prove your love.

- Listen to your intuition and pay attention to red flags. There were so many nights I would cry in my bed after a fight with Phil and yell out loud, "I can't do this anymore." That was my intuition telling me to stop the madness. For a long time, I didn't trust myself, God's plan for me, or what others kept telling me about my toxic partner. Pay attention to those who love you most, as they have your best interest at heart and can see what you cannot. If you find yourself defending the motives of the toxic person to others, you are in denial.

- Listen carefully to what your partner says about his past relationships. If he doesn't speak to any of his exes, or describes them all as crazy, run. If he never takes accountability for problems in his past, run. Toxic people don't have humility, don't apologize, and rarely take accountability for their mistakes. We all have some responsibility in our failed relationships. Listen to what he tells you in casual conversations about himself.

- Leave someone who makes you feel hard to love. If you find yourself questioning your own sanity and blaming yourself because he blames you, something is not right. I remember thinking and even saying aloud once to my toxic partner, "I don't think I've ever been with a man who makes me feel so loved, and then so hated." A person who truly loves you will never make you feel hated, despised, or as if they are disgusted with you. Healthy partners feel disappointment, irritation, and even anger, but never hatred. You are worthy of being loved unconditionally.

- If you think you are in a toxic and abusive relationship, reach out for help. There are typically resources both locally and nationally that will provide you with information and support. In the United States you can contact the Crisis Text Line: text HELLO to 741741 to connect with a Crisis Counselor, or call the National Domestic Violence Hotline: 1-800-799-7233.

Biography

All the names in the story have been changed. Elizabeth is in a good place today after doing the work necessary for healing. This included working with a counselor/life coach, studying emotional abuse, codependency, the strategies for healing, and finally, spiritual practices. She now helps women find their new normal after loss and live their life more euphorically. Elizabeth repaired the relationship with her children and they are all very close now. She was blessed to find and marry the second love of her life, whom her children embrace. Elizabeth's new husband, an emotionally healthy man and her equal, has inspired her to live an active lifestyle. They live by the motto "Life is short, play hard." They work remotely and split their time between the beach and the mountains. If you need support and life coaching, or just want to say hello, you can reach Elizabeth at: thehealisreal11@gmail.com.

FOURTEEN

Living a Pro-feminist Life
By Michael Flood

*It is by standing up for the rights of girls and women
that we truly measure up as men.*

—Desmond Tutu

I've happily worn my pro-feminist politics like a badge for nearly
twenty years. I joined an antisexist men's group at age twenty, did
Women's and Gender Studies at university, and completed a PhD in
Gender and Sexuality Studies. I founded the pro-feminist magazine
XY and ran it for seven years before turning it into a major website.
I continue to research issues of men, masculinity, and sexuality, and
I'm involved in activism and education particularly on men's violence
against women.

Writing all this makes me sound like I'm saying, "I'm so good.
I'm a pro-feminist guru." I don't believe that; I know that my own
efforts to be pro-feminist are as messy as anyone else's. Along the
way I've learned a lot, and I've made mistakes. But I have developed
a profound commitment to pro-feminism, and it has brought both

joys and challenges.

Becoming pro-feminist has been of profound personal benefit. Above all, it has shaped an inspired and confident sense of self, and it's deepened and strengthened my sexual and intimate involvements. I was probably going to be a happy and enthusiastic person anyway, but pro-feminism has sown my life with passion and purpose. I work as an academic at a university in Australia, doing research on men, gender, and violence. I have the fortune and privilege of doing work I enjoy, on issues with which I'm fascinated.

Pro-feminism also has enriched my relationships and friendships, and improved my emotional fluency and literacy. Part of the feminist critique of gender is a questioning of traditional masculine ways of being, including emotional incompetence and emotional constipation. I've become more adept both at hearing and expressing emotions, including vulnerable ones. Pro-feminism has enhanced my emotional skills, and that's been invaluable, whether I'm listening to a friend talk about a problem or nutting out a conflict with my partner.

Being pro-feminist means striving for egalitarian relations with women. And happily enough, that means better relationships as well. The evidence is that both women and men in egalitarian sexual relationships find more enjoyment and fulfillment than those in male-dominated relationships. And the sex is better, too. I treat my partner like a human being, ask or talk before taking sexual initiative, and treat her with respect and fairness, and all that builds emotional closeness and sexual intimacy.

Rejecting some traditionally masculine ways of relating has also enhanced my friendships. It has allowed greater intimacy than might have been possible had I held onto dominant ways of being male. Among heterosexual men, homophobia—fear and hostility toward gay men and lesbians—is the greatest threat to close friendships. Because I don't see male-male intimacy as suspect and I'm unafraid of being seen as gay, I've had more room to express tenderness and closeness.

It's often male friends who have helped me wrestle with the sticky questions of emotion, gender, and sexuality.

Many men's friendships with women are limited by the beliefs that women are of interest only as sexual objects and that close friendships with women are dangerously feminizing and homosexualizing. Instead, I've found friendships with women that are delightful, challenging, and playful. What is more, my involvement in feminist networks has helped me find a wider community of friends and allies. I've met lovely men who share a passion for social justice and change who've become buddies and mentors, and I've found connections with amazing and inspiring women. So, pro-feminism has brought the richness and joy of friendships, relationships, and political alliances with women and men.

Pro-feminist men support feminism first and foremost because we believe that we must. Given the fact of our unjust privilege, men have an ethical obligation to work to eliminate that privilege. There is a simple moral imperative that men give up their unjust share of power. But self-sacrificing altruism isn't a sufficient basis for a political movement, and there are obvious ways that men will benefit from supporting feminism and advancing toward gender equality. Men have a stake in a feminist future; feminism is also *for men*.

Men tend to pay heavy costs—in the form of shallow relationships, poor health, and early death—for conformity with narrow definitions of masculinity. Men and boys live in social relationships with women and girls, and the quality of every man's life depends to a large extent on the quality of those relationships. Many men who support efforts toward gender equality do so because of their concern, hopes, and love for the women in their lives. The communities in which men live benefit from gender reform, from flexibility in divisions of labor, improvements in women's health and well-being, and declines in male-to-male and male-to-female violence.

Being pro-feminist for me has meant trying to be a good person and working to change the world. These intertwined ethical goals capture the two central tasks for pro-feminist men: to live an ethical life, and to work toward a gender-equal society. Pro-feminism invites men to develop egalitarian relations with women and to avoid oppressive or abusive practices.

One of the key processes here is critical reflection: developing an awareness of the ways in which our actions and attitudes can be harmful to women and other men. Another is taking responsibility: acknowledging when we've made mistakes and making amends. A third is building an alternative, developing healthy and just ways of seeing and being.

Gender and gender inequalities saturate every area of our lives. Building gender justice requires personal change in all areas. For example, I've tried to ensure real consent in my sexual relations and to take or share responsibility for preventing pregnancy and disease. I use non-sexist language: I talk about "firefighters" and "access holes," not "firemen" and "manholes," and about finding someone to "chair" the meeting or "staff" (not "man") the stall, and I never use "bitch" or "woman" or "cocksucker" as insults. I share in the housecleaning and the washing up.

And in my relationship, I try to share the emotional division of labor too—by listening and empathizing, talking and sharing. I try not to fund or support sexist culture, such as films or music portraying girls or women in degrading or abusive ways. I support measures to promote equal opportunity in the workplace. I'm trying to raise my children in non-gender-stereotyped ways. I vote for political candidates and parties committed to gender equality, or at least less committed to propping up inequality.

Some of these changes have come pretty easily to me, as they fit within the broad orientation toward social justice I have long had. But others are harder. They involve reconstructing some of my deepest desires and attractions, consciously missing out on privileges I would otherwise be granted as a man, or taking on more of the burdens that otherwise would be lumped on women, such as domestic and caring work.

Individual strategies are important in making personal changes. I monitor and change my behavior, keep a diary in which I'm totally and brutally honest with myself, talk to friends and others, and read feminist works. But I've also found more collective strategies to be invaluable.

At age twenty I joined my first men's group. I'd gone to a public meeting for men advertised at a local community center, and I and a handful of other men with pro-feminist politics gravitated to one corner and ended up forming a men's antisexist consciousness-raising group. About eight of us met for three hours every week, for eighteen months until the group disbanded. Inspired by the classic feminist insight that "the personal is political," we explored a wide range of issues, from violence and pornography to homophobia and fathering.

As far as men's groups go, ours was unusual. It adopted explicitly pro-feminist politics, many of its members were young, and half were gay or bisexual. The group involved both substantial personal reflection and disclosure and some public political activism. For me it was a profound experience, and crucial to the formation of my passionate antisexist politics.

Making personal change can be complex, challenging, and cause ambivalence. There are certainly areas of my personal life I feel like I've pretty much sorted out, such as sexual consent. Through that early men's group, I'd realized that there were times when I'd used emotional blackmail and guilt to try to get my female partner to have sex. I'd not threatened her or ignored her refusals, but I would behave in a way that is on a continuum with other forms of sexual pressure and coercion. This was the most gut-wrenching of the revelations I had in that group, but an invaluable one. I've since developed a very strong commitment to sexual consent and respect, and a range of honest, playful, and sexy ways to negotiate consent in sexual interactions.

I've gotten better at doing my fair share of the housework. Issues of domestic labor were flagged for me early on. As a student, I was involved in a left-wing group on campus, and some of the women in the group asked, "Why is it always the women who are left to clean up after the meeting?" I also benefited from years of living in group houses with women.

My partner and I have been living together for six years now, and our domestic divisions of labor are pretty good. We used to have a rigid system of turn-taking for cooking and washing up, and this is still pretty fair. But I do find myself, in classically masculine fashion, sustaining some inequalities. For example, if I have cleaned the bathroom, several times over the next few days I'll mention how clean it looks, while not giving the same recognition to her efforts.

With a 15-month-old baby, domestic work has increased dramatically, and the domestic inequalities have worsened, as is typical in heterosexual couples. Negotiating our domestic divisions of labor is harder too, as broken nights' sleep makes us tired and grumpy. Becoming parents has made the work my partner does that I'd taken for granted more visible to me, and it's pushed me to pull my weight more.

The defining belief for pro-feminist men is that we have a responsibility to try to change our own sexist behaviors and attitudes and those of other men. There can never be a point at which a pro-feminist man says, "There, I've done it. I'm free of sexism." This is partly because our personal training in sexism is deep and complex, and there is always more we can do to build gender-just identities and relations. But it's also because no individual man can be free of sexism in a sexist society.

Men can rightly claim to be antisexist, but it is a mistake to claim to be non-sexist. In this patriarchal society, all men learn sexist thoughts and behaviors, all receive patriarchal privileges whether we want to or not, and all are complicit to some degree in sexism. Men can rid ourselves of particular sexist assumptions and behaviors, but in a sexist culture we will still receive patriarchal privileges. Our voices and beliefs will usually be given more authority, we will be assumed to be more competent and promotable workers than women, and we will experience levels of physical and sexual freedom denied to many women.

How does an everyday commitment to anti-sexism play out? I challenge male acquaintances' sexist remarks and jokes. I question them when they use sexist insults. I support female friends in naming the daily intrusions and harassments they experience or in recovering from abuse.

A few times I've tried to intervene when I've seen men assaulting women. The results of this are always the same. The man says, "It's none of your fucking business," he reacts with threats of violence, and you're left wondering if your intervention has done anything to lessen his violence. Still, this kind of intervention is important. It can slow down or stop the immediate violence already under way. It sends a message to the woman that others do not condone the violence she experiences and will try to support her. And it tells the man that at least one other man thinks his behavior is unacceptable. Most of my interventions into other men's sexist or abusive behavior are more low-key and involve far less risk of injury to myself. Typically, I'm risking social awkwardness and embarrassment at most.

The idea that feminism is anti-male is the most pernicious lie with which pro-feminist men must deal. Feminism is antisexist, not anti-male. Feminism is founded on a critique of the injustices and abuses of sexism. This critique is based on the fundamental belief that first, these inequalities are socially constructed, not biologically determined, and second, they can be changed. In fact, feminism would be meaningless without its hope—the fundamental belief that the relations between women and men can be democratic and liberatory.

Pro-feminist men, like feminist women, are not anti-male. We believe that men are perfectly capable of being loving, nurturing, and

non-oppressive human beings. We reject the idea that men are somehow intrinsically bad or oppressive. We are committed to enhancing
men's lives. We believe that men can change and we support every
man's efforts at positive change.

Despite all the reflection and all the experience I've described,
there are many things I need to change and things I need to watch
for. Gender relations are in a constant state of flux, and new forms
of inequality (and equality) emerge which pro-feminist men will
need to address. Examples include the "pornification" of mainstream
culture, shifts in workplace relations, and the energetic backlash by
anti-feminist men's groups.

Sexism is seductive. Men are constantly invited into forms of
domination over women. We're invited by advertising and pornography to see women only as objects and orifices. We're invited by male
acquaintances to let women's interests come second to ours: "Don't be
wrapped around her finger." Indeed, sometimes we're invited by women
themselves to be the one who makes the rules. Only good habits or
vigilance prevent us from accepting these invitations into inequality.
Either we resist because we live habitually gender-just lives in which
we see such behaviors as unthinkable or even incomprehensible, or
we resist because we recognize that here is a moment when we can
choose sexist inequality or justice, and we choose justice.

I've said that there are some areas of personal life in which I
feel like I've still got some work to do. One involves voyeurism and
objectification. In my mid-teens I amassed a collection of about fifty
soft-core porn magazines. I kept them hidden in my room, swapped
them with the boy next door, and of course, masturbated with them.

While using porn is now something I'd never do, I think this
early experience still influences my sexual desires. I continue to feel
attracted to the porno-style images of women I sometimes see, such
as on magazine covers, and I've been tempted to use porn when mas-
turbating. Doing an academic project on young people's exposure to

internet porn a couple of years ago, including documenting the range of sexual content that youth and adults alike can find online, didn't help. But this research also intensified my hostility to pornography; it showed me more clearly than ever how so much porn is built on contempt for women, and how some porn makes violence "sexy."

I know that pornography is not a simple issue for feminism. But for me, using porn does seem antithetical to the pro-feminism for which I stand. So, while it has been tempting sometimes to give in to the desires that still linger, I do not. Instead, I find other, more egalitarian and respectful ways to express sexual desire and experience sexual passion. I construct fantasies of mutual pleasure rather than using porn's fantasies of patriarchal domination. And when having sex, rather than imagining one of pornography's willing, grateful servant women, I open my eyes and engage with my partner as fully human. All this means that the sex I have does not leave me feeling soiled, guilty, and deadened, but connected, inspired, and alive.

Just as our deepest desires can be negatively shaped by social processes and experiences, they can also be shaped in positive ways. An important task for pro-feminism is to teach men to get off on equality: to be aroused by consent, respect, and mutual pleasure.

There is so much more that I could say about pro-feminism. While I've focused on personal change, participating in social activism is deeply personal, too. And some of the key challenges of pro-feminist men's activism—How do we engage and change "ordinary" men? How do we build alliances and partnerships with women? How do we deal with anti-feminist backlash?—are also deeply personal ones. But let me leave these questions for another day. There is much to do, and we have only just begun. Below are five tips for pro-feminist men.

- Do the personal work, putting your own house in order. Walk the walk, don't just talk the talk. But remember that you don't have to wait to be perfect before you can act.

- When you get it wrong, as we all inevitably do at some point, own it. Acknowledge your mistakes, make amends, and move on.
- Remind yourself of what you are *for*. Hold to your heart a positive feminist vision of a better world, and of how you and others benefit from progress toward gender equality.
- Be bold. Develop a passionate ethic that you can and will contribute to social change, guided by strong ideals and by connections to other advocates.
- Find and build communities of support, through friends, groups and networks. You can't go it alone. Make connections with other like-minded men and women so that your advocacy is not only sustainable but enjoyable.

Biography

Dr. Michael Flood is a researcher on men, masculinities, gender equality, and violence prevention. He is the author of the book *Engaging Men and Boys in Violence Prevention* (2019), and the lead editor of *Engaging Men in Building Gender Equality* (2015) and *The International Encyclopedia of Men and Masculinities* (2007). Michael is also an educator and advocate, with a long involvement in men's antiviolence work and pro-feminist activism. He runs the pro-feminist men's website www.xyonline.net. Note: This essay was first written in 2007.

FIFTEEN

Intersectionality and the Four Outcomes of Sexism

Sexism isn't a one-size-fits-all phenomenon. It doesn't happen to black and white women the same way.

—Kimberlé Crenshaw

Jane is a Black woman who has been in the workforce for ten years. After discussions with coworkers, she realized that her salary was not only significantly less than the white men in the company in similar positions, but it was also less than the white women in similar roles. One colleague, a white female who started working at the company when Jane did, made 20 percent more than Jane. Jane talked with a few other Black women at her company and realized they were all paid less than white women in the same jobs.

Alice was laid off from her job when she was 60 years old. She spent over a year job hunting before she was hired for a job that paid 25 percent less than what she had been making in her previous role. While job hunting, she received advice to remove twenty years of work history from her résumé. When interviewing, she was frequently asked how much longer she planned on working. Jane believed that her gray hair was a liability when interviewing in person. She felt that even though she had extensive expertise, she was viewed as less competent and marketable because of her age.

Megan had difficulties paying attention her entire life, both at school and at work. She met with several doctors throughout her life. She was finally diagnosed with attention-deficit/hyperactivity disorder (ADHD) as an adult. Megan wondered why she hadn't been diagnosed sooner. She learned that while ADHD is a well-known disability, it was initially thought of as a disability that only occurred in men. The testing and research for the disease were conducted with men, and the diagnosis was written about men's symptoms. Megan wished women had been included in the testing and analysis.

The *Oxford English Dictionary* defines intersectionality as "the interconnected nature of social categorizations such as race, class, and gender as they apply to a given individual or group, regarded as creating overlapping and interdependent systems of discrimination or disadvantage." Kimberlé Crenshaw first coined the term intersectionality in 1989, and it was added to the *Oxford English Dictionary* in 2015.

Its importance is increasingly recognized in the women's rights arena. Intersectionality is the acknowledgment that everyone has unique experiences of biases and discrimination. A 30-year-old non-disabled white woman's experiences will differ from those of a Black woman, a 60-year-old white woman, or a woman with a disability. Jane, Alice, and Megan all experienced sexism differently when it intersected with other biases.

Four Outcomes of Sexism and Intersectionality

The four outcomes of sexism have an intersectionality overlay. Sexist microaggression, discrimination, harassment, and violence can impact women differently based on other types of bias they might experience combined with sexism. Many biases can intersect with sexism, including racism, ageism, ableism, sizeism, classism, and sexuality. The intersection of sexism with racism, ageism, and ableism will be further explored in this chapter.

While the overlay of intersectionality is critical to the sexism discussion, it's essential to keep the road map to being antisexist simple. First, approach an incidence of sexism from the lens of one of the four outcomes of sexism, then apply an intersectionality lens to the issue and ask if another bias is involved as well. Microaggression, discrimination, harassment, and violence toward women and girls are often greater when intersectionality exists.

FOUR OUTCOMES OF SEXISM	
Microaggression	**Discrimination**
Sexist Language	Education
Stereotypes	Employment
Objectification	Wage Gap
Shaming	Career
Mansplaining	Healthcare
Invalidation	Sexual
Harassment	**Violence**
Verbal	Physical
Physical	Sexual
Online	Emotional
Bullying	Economic
Street	Coercive Control
Flashing	Femicide

The Intersection of Sexism and Racism

Women of color face disproportionately high barriers both on and off the job. They tend to experience more microaggressions and are more likely to be subjected to disrespectful comments and behavior. They are impacted by human resource-process biases, including hiring and promotions. Women of color are less likely than other groups of women to receive positive feedback on their leadership skills even when their overall performance ratings are good. They tend to have fewer interactions with senior leadership and are less likely to be viewed as individuals at work.

The gender wage gap is an essential measure of equity. The data show that women of color have the most significant gaps in wages when compared with male colleagues. This can be explained by the underevaluation of work supplied by women, particularly women of color. In the United States, women on average earned just 83 cents for every dollar earned by white, non-Hispanic men. Still, this aggregate number provides an incomplete picture. For every dollar earned by white, non-Hispanic men, Hispanic women earned 57 cents, Native American women earned 60 cents, and Black women earned 64 cents.

The amount lost because of the pay gap compounds over time. Over a forty-year career, it can add up to approximately one million dollars. Many factors that contribute to the gender wage gap, including jobs and hours worked, can be attributed to sexism and racism.

Women of color may experience a higher rate of harassment and violence, much of which can be attributed to the intersection of sexism and racism. Eight people were murdered in the attack on spas in Atlanta, Georgia; six were Asian women. Asian women have been portrayed as submissive, hypersexual, and exotic for centuries. The few Asian women portrayed in the media, including books and movies, have often been shown in those stereotypical roles. Those stereotypes can lead to misogyny, racism, and femicide. They can have the effect of excusing and normalizing violence toward Asian women. Data about anti-Asian attacks show that Asian women are twice as likely to report experiencing attacks and harassment as men.

Women who are the only people of their race and gender in a room at work have what is referred to as "double jeopardy." They tend to be more heavily scrutinized and feel as if their performance is put under a microscope. They often encounter comments and behavior that leave them feeling excluded. Women at the intersection of sexism and racism often face more bias, discrimination, and pressure to perform. The intersection of racism and sexism can include different experiences depending on the women's race.

> *I feel like I've had to work harder and do more to prove myself compared to my colleagues. I think the bar for me is higher when getting recognized. I believe I have this reputation of doing whatever it takes to fix a problem. They expect that I will work myself to death to get something done. The expectations are different. It is very stressful. The average person has no idea about the stress that women of color experience. They have no idea about the small ways that women of color get stereotyped and demeaned that make them feel less than. It happens all the time.*
>
> **—Kyoko, United States**

The Intersection of Sexism and Ageism

Significantly more women than men report that they have experienced ageism. One research study reported that 72 percent of women between 45 and 74 said they think people experience age discrimination at work. Only 57 percent of men in the same age range said the same. Younger and older women can experience biases at the intersection of sexism and ageism. Younger women may experience microaggressions related to their ability to do the job because they are perceived as too young. They can be subjected to various forms of harassment if they appear more vulnerable because of their youth. It's often young women who become involved in abusive relationships with older men.

Older women say they've experienced ageism during the job search, and most commonly faced ageism during initial screening conversations, hiring decisions, and in-person interviews. Many older women have tried to conceal their age during the hiring process, including interviews. Some limit their work experience to the last twenty years or try to look younger. As women show visible signs of aging, they believe they are viewed as less competent. They feel invisible and isolated even though they have a great deal of expertise. Few companies include a focus on the intersection of sexism and age in their diversity, equity, and inclusion initiatives. Age discrimination often goes unaddressed because of the way society views older women.

Women are judged first on their appearance, before ability and experience. They are held to a far higher standard than men because of sexism. It's a stereotypical standard of femininity that embraces youth. Society and the media present men as aging gracefully, and their gray hair is considered distinguished. Women are no longer considered of value when they age, and gray hair signals that it's time for them to become silent and disappear. There is a saying, a sexist microaggression, "Men age like wine and women age like milk."

Research shows that many women are disadvantaged financially as they age due to the wage and work gaps they experienced by taking time away from formal jobs to raise children. While the negative attitude about women aging is slowly changing as the population of older women grows, the biases still exist and have a significant impact.

Age discrimination was why Julianne Taaffe and Kathryn Moon sued Ohio State University, a case that was settled when the two educators were awarded $765,000 in back pay, benefits, and legal fees. Another win for the two women was that the university agreed to review its policies for preventing and investigating age discrimination. Kathryn was 64 when the complaint was filed and had worked as an ESL instructor for 31 years at the university. Julianne was 59 and had worked at the school for more than 20 years. An ESL director was quoted in the lawsuit as saying that trying to get older teachers to modernize was like "herding hippos," among other insults that were sexist microaggressions.

I had just set up a call center for my employer when I was laid off at age 55. I decided to take some time off to travel and write a book. One year later, I sent out my résumé filled with excellent work experience and got no replies. I believe it was because I was over 55. I had also let my hair turn to its natural gray color. When I finally got an interview invitation, I could see a change in the interviewers' expressions when they saw my gray hair and wrinkles. The conversation was kept very short. The questions I was asked were less about my experience and more about how long I planned to keep working, as if my life was over. It felt like just as I was hitting my stride, I got hit with ageism on top of sexism.

—**Jenny, Australia**

The Intersection of Sexism and Ableism

Disabilities can take many forms, including impaired hearing or vision, paralysis, pain, chronic illness, learning disabilities, and mental health diagnoses. According to the United Nations, women and girls with any form of disability are generally among the more vulnerable and marginalized in society. About one in ten working women have a disability that makes their experiences at work more difficult. Women with disabilities reported that they are often overlooked, undervalued, and interrupted. They are more frequently accused of being too angry or emotional. Women with disabilities indicated they don't have equal opportunities for raises and promotions.

Many ableist microaggressions are essential to recognize, as they insult women with disabilities. These are a few that have become normalized.

- That's so lame.
- You are retarded.
- That guy is crazy.

- You're acting so bipolar today.
- Are you off your meds?
- It's like the blind leading the blind.

Women with disabilities tend to face more microaggression, discrimination, harassment, and violence than women with other types of intersections with sexism. The global literacy rate for women with disabilities is less than 1 percent. They often have difficulty with physical access to healthcare and are more susceptible to violence, poverty, and dislocation. Sexual assault rates are high for all women but significantly higher for those with disabilities. One study stated that 83 percent of women with disabilities experience sexual assault during their lifetime. They face significant barriers in accessing adequate housing and related services. They are more likely to be institutionalized than men with disabilities.

Sarah, a young woman with a learning disability, became trapped in a relationship that involved coercive control. Sarah's partner moved into her apartment very quickly after they met. He offered to take care of the bills using a joint account and said she shouldn't be in charge of the money because of her learning disability. At first, Sarah enjoyed having a boyfriend and felt normal because of it. But he soon started abusing her, calling her stupid. He took out a loan in her name and kept her from seeing her mother.

The neighbors began calling the police because Sarah's boyfriend was making a lot of noise and intimidating the neighbors. Sarah ended the relationship after five years, but he kept turning up at the apartment. He would bang on the door, threaten her, and turn up at the grocery store when she was there. Sarah ended up filing a complaint with the police after her ex-boyfriend broke down her front door.

I've been in my current job for ten years. I show up, work hard, and accomplish my job objectives. I take on extra work and get involved in other work activities. I keep applying for jobs that would result in a promotion and job rotations. I've never gotten one, and I'm just so discouraged. I feel like nobody wants me because of my disability, and no one thinks I deserve anything better. I dream of working for a company that welcomes me as a person with a disability. A company where I can excel and be successful. That's my dream, and it shouldn't be a dream. It should be a normal part of my working life.

—**Melanie, Canada**

Allyship

Allyship plays an integral part in eliminating microaggression, discrimination, harassment, and violence toward women and girls. Allyship is the role of a person who advocates and actively works to include a marginalized group in all areas of society, not as a member of that group but in solidarity with members and their struggle. Men and women can be allies to women who are struggling for equality.

Men supporting women as allies is critical for the success of women who experience multiple biases. Allies aren't looking to be called allies. It's not about being labeled; it's about taking action. Within organizations, allyship is a strategic tool used to increase women's hiring, retention, and promotion. Allies can be advocates for systemic change in any process, program, or policy that promotes sexism and gender inequality, including government legislation.

When more privileged colleagues support women as allies, it can significantly change their experiences. Women have reported that when they have strong allies at work, they are happier in their jobs, less likely to be burned out, and less likely to leave their companies. While many white employees consider themselves allies of women of color at work, far fewer are taking allyship actions. White allies need to be accomplices, take risks, and actively confront bias and discrimination against all women. Allies need to support women who experience sexism intersecting with other biases because they experience higher rates of discrimination. When women who experience multiple biases attempt to speak up, they often experience retaliation.

Women want allies who advocate for new opportunities for them at work. They need allies, in particular male allies, to be mentors or sponsors. Allies should confront discrimination against women and specifically stand up for women experiencing multiple biases. Allies need to publicly acknowledge women for their ideas at work and include women when making decisions. Allies should educate themselves about women's experiences and the impacts of different types of intersectionality on women. Allies are the change agents who drive systemic change to policies, practices, and culture both inside and outside organizations.

> *After my divorce, I became a single parent to two young daughters for over a year until I fell in love with a beautiful Black woman and married again. I found myself in a "yours, mine, and ours" blended family where, as a white man, I could see how women were marginalized and not expected to have successful, well-paying careers. They lived lives where their voices didn't matter. With the love and support of my wife, we encouraged and empowered our daughters to dream big and shoot for the stars. They are both married now with children and successful careers. They realize the power of their voices as successful women in the world, and my wife and I couldn't be prouder of them both.*
>
> **—Bob, United States**

Challenge Sexism, Champion Women's Rights, and Create Equality

Following is a list of actions that men and women can take to create stronger allyship and be antisexist. Review the list and add activities to your Antisexist Action Plan.

It doesn't matter how involved you are in women's rights and how hard you work to be antisexist; you can continually strengthen your skills to be a better intersectional ally or accomplice. Anyone with privilege in an area can be an ally to someone without privilege in that area. Here are a few ideas to improve your allyship.

- Check your privilege. All your social identities contribute to your privilege. Consider how your privilege impacts the discrimination you do and don't experience.
- Listen and learn about women's views about intersectionality, where sexism intersects with other biases. Read and research.
- Make space for women to speak about their experiences of microaggression, discrimination, harassment, or violence. Don't speak for them, and don't speak over them.
- Watch your language; microaggression quickly becomes normalized. Many of the words we use daily are sexist, exclusionary, and offensive to women.
- Become aware of other biases and how they affect microaggression.
- Get comfortable with being uncomfortable. Learning about the challenges that women face may cause feelings of self-blame.
- Confront microaggression, discrimination, and harassment when you see it.
- Identify a woman with whom you can build a supportive partnership. Women want support in the form of mentors and sponsors that will advocate for them when new opportunities arise.
- Challenge the status quo. Find ways to be a change agent who drives systemic change to policies, practices, programs, and culture both inside and outside of organizations.

- Become a public ally, challenge sexism, champion women's rights, and create equality.

The best allies are not always who you think they might be. Allyship can come in many forms. Allies can be people at work or in your network. They might be family members or customers. People you recently met and connected with could be good allies. As you look for allies, remember, there is power in numbers.

- Look for allies who have demonstrated support of diversity, equity, and inclusion.
- Find allies who have mentored other women.
- Locate allies that are educated about sexism and intersectionality.
- Discover if potential allies have advocated for women and other minorities.
- Engage with potential and actual allies regularly to build relationships.
- Have open and honest conversations with your allies.
- Be realistic about the level of support you can expect.
- Don't take offense if an ally has to say no to a request.

SIXTEEN

Ally or Accomplice
By Carla Haskins

We can disagree and still love each other unless your disagreement is rooted in my oppression and denial of my humanity and right to exist.

—Robert Jones, Jr.

When I was thirty years old, I made a life-altering decision to move across the country to pursue a career opportunity. My goal was to climb the corporate ladder and achieve success. I was my ancestors' wildest dream. A descendant of slaves and a product of the civil rights experiment. As a Black woman, I knew I would face unique challenges, but there was so much I didn't yet understand about what I would face in environments and spaces as a Black woman. I wasn't ready for the complexity of living that dual reality and only gradually began to understand what it meant with each promotion in the corporate world.

Reflecting back on those early years, there was this duality of my existence I instinctively understood I would have to learn to navigate at all times. It's not something they train you for in college. There was, and still is, the tension of navigating these two worlds, of being Black and a woman, the intersection of these anchors and how they affected my experiences in the workplace.

I felt like I was constantly wrangling with the ever-present reality of racism and warring against the dynamics of being a working professional woman caught in the vortex of tradition and expectations attached to my gender. Of all the things I thought I was prepared for, this dynamic and duality of Black womanhood with a foot in both worlds at the intersection of race and gender was not one of them.

I'm a child of the seventies, born in 1970. A mere fifteen years after the Montgomery bus boycott, only seven years before the March on Washington where Dr. Martin Luther King Jr. delivered his iconic "I Have a Dream" speech, six years before the Civil Rights Act of 1964 and an era of federal legislation for Black Americans, including voting rights, equal housing protections, and access to quality education. It still blows my mind when I think about the historical implications and timing of my life's story.

Because I tested out of the first grade and my local elementary school was deemed inadequate to meet my educational needs, I was accepted into and bussed to an elementary school magnet program that accelerated my educational opportunities. It was desegregation bussing, also known as forced bussing. The same type of bussing Vice President Kamala Harris experienced as a child when she was transported to a school in a different neighborhood to address racial segregation.

Access to better education paved the way for me to be exposed to people from all cultures for the first time in my life. I remember my elementary classmates vividly. All shades, shapes, and sizes. Incredibly diverse. It was overall a very positive experience. Recently it dawned on me that since that time, I've yet to experience the same level of diversity and variety. I had become accustomed to going to school and interacting with children and teachers from other cultures, but my home life was an entirely Black cultural experience.

Forgetting I was Black could be dangerous. Growing up in the South was a primarily segregated experience, publicly and privately. It was and some would argue still is a way of life. Federal and state legislation didn't suddenly change deeply rooted social customs and practices that had been in place for generations, for both Black and white people. It's just the way it was, and I never thought twice about it.

By the time I entered college, I had started to put the pieces together. I attended a state school and what Black people have termed a PWI, a predominantly white institution. I dove even more deeply into American history, the African diaspora, and became involved in student activism as part of the Black Student Union. For the first time, my eyes began to open to how things worked for the majority culture and how my personal story fit into it. It was an incredibly transformative time in my life. I began to understand the gaping holes of inequity and systemic racism, including the wealth gap, the education gap, and the health gap.

College is where I first heard the term "twofer" used to refer to me. I was Black and a woman. You got two for one if you hired me, accepted me, and promoted me. It was an excellent way for corporations to hit that diversity quota. College was also the place I first felt my Blackness stood out, loud and clear, every day, all day.

I had large classes as a freshman where I was one of maybe three Black students in a class with over four hundred students. It's where I first learned to scan the space for other Black people as soon as I entered any room. I was always outnumbered. I never felt entirely safe and was constantly on guard. I learned how to survive in a place that wasn't built for me, which accommodated my existence but did not welcome me.

After college, my awareness of the world and how I fit into it was very different. The first female executives I worked for were white. They were incredibly thoughtful and aware of how I added to the team, meaning they fully understood my presence. They were my advocates, publicly supportive of me and understanding of policy, but not at all ready to go out on any personal limb to effect change.

I recall applying for an opportunity I was well qualified for within another division and not only being told "it's not your turn" but also being made to feel I was disloyal for even thinking about it. I was asked to take a management role in an affluent, highly desirable location that had never hired a Black or person of color to lead it. When I refused to accept the role (which came with a pay cut), I soon realized they considered me uncompliant because I refused to allow them to control my career path and placement for their diversity efforts. So, I left.

As I began to work in different environments, I began to note the critical differences in my life's parameters compared to my white colleagues. For example, I was being exposed to the personal lives of my white colleagues, both male and female, and noting to myself how different their economic pressure, or lack of stress, was from mine. Work, for most of them, was optional.

For white men it was normal to be the sole financial provider in their homes. I recognize I was traveling in a particular orbit, so it's not indicative of all white women or white men and their experience. The notable differences in their choices to support their spouse's ability to stay home with their children, or for women to have the option not to return to work immediately after giving birth, were remarkable to me. For most Black women there isn't that option for reasons directly attributable to systemic racism and the dismantling of the Black family as a by-product of slavery in the United States.

By the time I made it to the lead in various roles and made it to the executive realm, it often felt like college again, isolating and unsafe. To be honest, I don't think they even understood how embedded white male leadership can be toxic and exhausting for anyone not like them who sits at their table. On the whole, men tended to be less aware and even less understanding of leading with a Black executive who is also a woman as well as the implications of that dynamic.

Remember my reference to "twofer"? I came to expect the male-oriented jokes and comments, how awkward it felt at times when the conversation turned to racism and issues that affected women, and rarely being asked my perspective. I learned to speak up, not just for myself, but for others. I was always outnumbered and outvoted. My presence was accepted and tolerated, not celebrated.

Allyship is a massive buzzword in the aftermath of George Floyd. We all witnessed a time of global mobilization around needed changes in American policing that resonated worldwide. His murder also was a spark for conversations around allyship and what it means for non-Black, specifically white people, in positions of power to effect change.

I began to understand that any expectation of allyship from white colleagues was always on their terms. And allyship alone is not enough. Allyship has to go beyond just building relationships and learning; it must lead to action as well. My relationships with white women and men were generally acceptable until I brought to light specific concerns and action steps around racism and sexism.

In my experience, white people easily tire of the conversation, and please don't expect them to make changes that impact them personally or professionally. White women and Black women live vastly different experiences in the workplace, and rarely do we connect on issues we share, and more importantly, on issues we don't. White women have the luxury of focusing on issues that affect their womanhood and sexuality. In my experience, if they will be economically or socially affected, all bets are off, and allyship goes out the window. It's challenging even for me; how do I handle the intersections I blatantly represent? Do I focus on being Black or do I focus on being a woman? How can I possibly choose? Do I have a choice, though? No. A resounding no.

The questions and consequences of considering allyship are vast and complex. I get it. But that's change, right? Change comes with a cost. The murder of George Floyd in 2020 changed me forever.

Change in the racist and sexist ecosystems we have gotten so well adjusted to is more urgent than ever. I am more impatient than ever for the lives of Black people and especially Black women to change.

I got so tired of hearing the words "ally" and "allyship." It signals comfort and complicity to me while Black men and women continue to fight for our lives and the lives of our children. So, allow me to challenge us all, women and men, with some action steps regarding understanding the intersection of race and gender.

- Move from being an ally to an accomplice. In a court of law, the word "accomplice" has a negative connotation, as in someone who has assisted someone else in wrongdoing. In the context of gender and social justice work, an accomplice is someone who helps others to create a space of inclusion, equity, and safety for all, often at the risk of their own social and professional standing and physical well-being. I firmly believe the era of just being an ally is over. As a Black woman, please hear me; it's not enough. Black women need accomplices who share the risk and are willing to fight with us for this change. Based on the history of the feminist movement, white women have to understand and acknowledge the role they play in the barriers Black women face. Do I need to detail the privilege white men exist to enjoy? How will you use your power and privilege to change the structures and systems that keep gender and racial inequity in place?
- Be honest with yourself about where you stand on the intersection of race and gender issues. Ask yourself how far you're willing to go with those convictions to effect change. What choices will you make? It's one thing to have a moral position and another dynamic to change areas of your life to reflect those convictions. It's okay to be committed to journeying through the change, but I implore you to first count the costs, because it will

cost you. If the outworking of racial and gender equity is not embedded in the fabric of your personal and professional lives, you are giving these life-and-death issues nothing more than lip service. It's better to be a learner than to be disingenuous when it comes time to put action behind your convictions.

- We've all heard that white people should be learning and listening more than ever. Yes, and yes again. The whole truth about the history of American slavery and the stories of Black women and the Black family have been intentionally buried. I believe there is an attack on the truth to deceive future generations and to desensitize us to what happened to African Americans in the United States. It is up to us to listen, learn, hold those truths closely, and engage the next generation to continue to empower change beyond ourselves. Systemic racism runs deep and wide. Once you've learned and listened, learn and hear more and DO. Let me be super clear. The onus of this work lies with white people, who have the social and economic power to change systems they didn't create, but whose benefits they continue to enjoy.

- Teach and expose your children to the truth. How does this problem seem to only get bigger with each generation? As the saying goes, "The only thing necessary for the triumph of evil is for good men to do nothing." I firmly believe our children, our sons and daughters, learn a lot from what we *don't* do. They are paying just as much attention to the decisions we don't make as to those we do. They see us. What are we teaching them about the equality of women and the inequalities Black people face? Will they choose the sidelines or will they choose to become change agents? Will they see you quit when it gets uncomfortable? Will they witness your participation in change only until it's no longer economically or socially convenient?

- Exercise the courage to confront. I don't think any of us are born with courage, but we build or erode it with every choice we make. We need courageous leadership at every turn, in our homes, neighborhoods, workplaces, schools, government, and places of worship. It starts with you. If you see something, say something. You are often in conversations and situations that allow racism and sexism to thrive. Your silence is complicity. How will you know when it's time to make a courageous decision? You'll know. You'll feel it in your gut. I hope it nags at you and steals your sleep until you do the right thing.

I won't ever forget the period after George Floyd's murder. A white male colleague told me he was raised by a Black woman. He attempted to connect with me, to make me feel like he genuinely understood or that he saw me as a Black woman, because of this affinity for the woman who took care of him. It was a slap in the face. He had no clue he had just fallen into a gaping ditch of ignorance. I was enraged that he had no idea of the racist, sexist, and historical significance of saying that to me. I fully understood what he was saying, and it didn't feel like a microaggression at all but a full-on attack on my Blackness and my womanhood.

My very humanity felt threatened. It was as if he was reminding me of my place and his. No matter how much success you have or what promotions you experience, don't ever forget I have the power. Not only was I in shock but I was traumatized, exhausted, and highly disheartened. Exhausted because it was a stabbing reminder of how much work white men and women need to do to dig us all out of this ditch of sexism and racism. It was also disheartening because I realized in all my years of living this dichotomy of racism and sexism, I had seen little to no change. It felt like a huge gut punch and a giant leap backward.

My mother had always instilled in me that education would be my only way out. I believe that's true, but that's not the whole story. Higher education for Black women is also a way in. A way into the spaces and places where we learn to acclimate to survive. We know to adjust so we are less threatening to white people. We sometimes take on the ways of oppression to be accepted, get the job, advance, and be promoted. Often at the expense of ourselves. At the expense of our Blackness. At the cost of losing ourselves to survive in spaces that never intended us to be there.

Many white people don't participate in the power exchange that breaking down racist structures will create because they are too focused on what they will lose. But have you considered what you will gain? Imagine what we could achieve if we are genuinely in this together, as accomplices, sharing risk and reward in the fight against sexism and racism.

Biography

Carla Haskins is a multigifted and accomplished speaker and writer. Her career portfolio spans both the for-profit and non-profit sectors, with experience in human resources, publishing, content development, and diversity and belonging initiatives. She is a self-proclaimed wordsmith, word nerd, and bibliophile. Carla is pursuing graduate study in Clinical Mental Health counseling and writes to stay sane. Not much makes her happier than to be left alone for hours in dusty old bookstores with piles of vintage books. She lives in Texas with her husband, Ed.

SEVENTEEN

Female, Disabled . . . and Dating

By Shaina Ghuraya

Loving this body should not be a radical act.

—CAITLYN SIEHL

Growing up as an Indian girl, there was one thing my uncles and aunties loved to talk about: getting all of us kids married off. But they had a tendency to ignore the elephant in the room, or rather the young girl in a 300-pound wheelchair.

I was born with spinal muscular atrophy, which meant I would be in an electric wheelchair for the rest of my life. It also apparently meant that I would never get married or have kids, the only way to happiness according to many of my conservative relatives. This was never explicitly stated, but when nobody jokes about getting you married off or your wedding day, it's very much implied.

Despite this, I had a fairly normal childhood growing up, and a large part of that was due to my parents. To their credit, they tried to fight back against societal prejudices and discriminatory relatives. My own grandmother thought I should be confined to my room for the rest of my days, something she no longer thinks. Though my parents had fairly progressive views about disability, even they never thought I would date or have any type of romantic life. Between them, my relatives, and society as a whole, a self-fulfilling prophecy was created. They conditioned me to the point where I forced myself to be asexual and to not want a partner, because it was too painful to confront the fact that I wanted a romantic life but could not attain it.

My life throughout middle and high school, and some of college, was one of complete devotion to my studies. I am very much a workaholic, even to this day, because the work is a distraction and temporarily fills the romantic void in my life. It also didn't help that I didn't feel like a woman. Girls in high school were growing up and wearing makeup, and I felt like an impostor when I tried to get done up. I wanted to feel beautiful, but with hardly any portrayals in the media of women with disabilities being considered "beautiful" or "sexy," it was hard. I surrounded myself with loyal friends who would literally go to the ends of the earth for me. It was the closest I would allow myself to get to people, terrified to have anything beyond a friendship lest it not work out.

It wasn't until my second year of college that a guy took interest in me, and it simultaneously scared and excited me. I kept it a secret from my parents, and at the time I told myself it was because they probably wouldn't want me, their daughter, dating. As an Indian woman I had been told that girls should never date in college, or ever for that matter. But as the relationship went on, I realized that I didn't tell them because I didn't want them to know if we broke up. I didn't want them to know that their prophecy was true.

The relationship was good, and he was a great guy, and he did help me feel pretty. But at the end of the day, there was this nagging voice in the back of my head that said that I shouldn't have a boyfriend. I remember sitting at a restaurant on Valentine's Day with him, and all the other couples were able-bodied. Everything I had been conditioned to believe just came rushing back. In the coming weeks I became more and more closed off, and we eventually broke up.

After that, I thought I was happy. I had my safe life filled with work and school back. That was all I needed. And I again tried to make myself fit into this asexual identity, but I didn't push away the idea of wanting a partner. It took me a couple of years after that to explore my own sexual identity and realize that I was not in fact asexual, but that I had some serious self-hate to overcome. I thought it was wrong for me to want a heterosexual relationship, and was ashamed of it, because I was ashamed of myself. It took months of reconditioning my thought process to get over this, and I'm still working on it.

There were a couple of things that helped me recondition my thought process. One was being surrounded by people who are very progressive in every sense of the word. I am a filmmaker, and when I attended film school I was surrounded by a cohort of incredibly diverse people where no one relationship was the same for those who were in relationships. My family is very cookie-cutter, and I always felt that me being in any relationship would crack their cookie-cutter world.

It especially scared me when I thought that the only person I could be in a relationship with would be another person in a wheelchair. I had my own ableism to confront with that notion. I just couldn't see my normal family being accepting of two people in wheelchairs having a romantic relationship. Being able to immerse myself in a community of people who accepted me for who I was really helped boost my confidence.

The second thing that helped was putting myself on online dating sites, which my fellow students helped me do. Being honest about my disability and seeing how many people were genuinely interested in me was another huge confidence booster. I completely broke down that first day, realizing how much of my time I had wasted believing that nobody would want me romantically and that I was unworthy of love.

My latest serious relationship was good, but again I had some issues to overcome. Even though I was more comfortable and happier with myself, I now had this mindset of needing to cling to this relationship because this guy was the only one who could love me. I stayed in it knowing that he wasn't right for me until I gained the courage, with plenty of help from my friends, to break it off.

But despite these strides, there are still obstacles, and the biggest one is the career I'm going into. As a person who eventually wants to be a showrunner, I have to immerse myself in the shows coming out of Hollywood. Although visibility is much better for men with disabilities, there's still hardly any for women with disabilities. That is an indication of how society views men versus women. Mainstream shows such as *Superstore*, *Speechless*, *Family Guy*, *Glee*, and *The Office* all portray men with disabilities, and they show them having active romantic and sometimes sexual lives.

But perhaps the show that does the best job of putting men versus women with disabilities into perspective is Marvel's TV show *Daredevil*. In flashbacks to protagonist Matt Murdock's college life, he is shown as being the one who gets all the ladies because he has a tragic story and is blind, earning him their sympathies. The show alludes to the disability actually making him more desirable since it makes women think he has a sensitive side.

The lack of portrayals of women with disabilities in media is really the issue here, and a large part of it is definitely because of ridiculously unattainable beauty standards that women with disabilities don't fit. Eventually I'll be in a position of power where I can make female-driven inclusive and diverse content, and hopefully this wave of inclusion in the media will make great progress in remedying this.

The other obstacle that I was made aware of is that, according to the University of Michigan, it is estimated that as many as 40 percent of women with disabilities experience sexual assault or physical violence in their lifetimes. This is terrifying, especially for a woman in my position where I quite literally cannot do anything if I am taken out of my chair. It's a huge barrier for women to overcome, and I hope the suggestions below will provide some structure to prevent this from happening.

I am currently single, but I am open to dating and finding love, and I am much more confident in myself. I even got over my own prejudices and have since been more than willing to date people with disabilities. I know what I want, and I'm not afraid to put myself out there. I was my own worst enemy for the longest time, sabotaging my efforts at finding a partner. Don't get me wrong, being in a wheelchair and dating still is not easy. I'm not getting tons of guys lining up, but I only need one.

I hope my advice and clear steps below can help you, as a woman, gain confidence to love yourself and feel worthy of being loved.

- Find your cheerleaders. Surround yourself with people who accept you unconditionally and help build you up for who you are rather than try to change you. Now with social media we are more connected than ever, and it can be a great tool to find friends who will help you love yourself. It's also really important to keep these friends in the loop on who you are dating and when you are out with that person for safety reasons. If you're not in a great relationship, your personality is going to change and they will probably know something is wrong.

- Cut the toxic people from your life. This is harder to do, because sometimes they are the only people you have, or they're family. That is why finding your tribe first is important, so that you don't feel like you are alone once you end the toxic relationships. Even limiting your interactions with people who do not accept you for who you are is a step in the right direction. Recognizing and cutting out toxic relationships will help you identify when you're with people who might be toxic themselves.

- Follow sex-positive people on social media. There are so many female disability advocates online now. Last year I followed some that actively talk about and post pictures of their inter-abled relationships. And just seeing pictures of them every day in *healthy* relationships helped to normalize the idea of an inter-abled relationship in my mind. I even had my ex-boyfriend follow those accounts so that he could not only get used to the idea but become more educated about dating someone with a disability.

- If you can, please see a therapist. Therapy helped me a lot, though I wasn't able to have as many sessions as I'd hoped. I waited till I was getting my MFA to get help, and that was because I had this stubborn irrational mindset of not wanting a therapist to assume I was coming in to talk about problems relating to my disability. Having friends that openly talked about therapy helped, and in the end, they held me accountable and even walked with me to the therapist's office so I couldn't back out.

- Put yourself out there. It's scary, and terrifying, but make a profile on a dating site. If it helps, have friends hold you accountable to doing this, and even have them help you write it. Sometimes they can see you more clearly than you can see yourself. Please be honest and upfront about your disability. Do not hide it. Once it's up, take it slow. See how many people like your profile and want to get to know you. One thing I did when starting out was I only messaged guys who liked me first, since I didn't feel confident enough to go after a guy online. I wanted him to make the first move. I'm still working on finding the courage to swipe right on guys who haven't already liked my profile.

- Go on a date, even if you don't really think the guy is the right one for you. If he is sweet and kind and you feel safe, arrange for a date in a public place. Dating with a disability is terrifying, and I found myself texting guys but ultimately coming up with nitpicky excuses to not go on dates with them because I was scared. I had these irrational thoughts that everyone at the restaurant or coffee shop would be staring and wondering how I could be on a date. It's silly, I know. Going on a couple of first dates will help you realize that you can in fact get through them, and it'll help you be more confident and open when the right person eventually comes along.

- Don't give up, and make sure to keep surrounding yourself with great people. We are all worthy of love.

Biography

Shaina Ghuraya is a graduate student of the University of Southern California's Master of Fine Arts program in Film and Television production. She grew up in the suburb of Elk Grove in California, and began her journey as a political science major in order to become an activist for people with disabilities such as herself. When she saw the changes that were implemented as a result of a film she made documenting the inaccessibility issues at her undergraduate college, she began pursuing media production. Her film *Wheelchair Wendy* screened at ReelAbilities Film Festival and was featured on *LA This Week*. She has since started a production company with her friends called Rebuilt Minds to promote diversity on screen in hopes of shaping a more inclusive and empathetic world. Her work can be seen on her YouTube page, https://bit.ly/Rebuiltminds, and the company's website is rebuiltminds.com. She can be contacted at shainaghuraya@gmail.com or on her Instagram @disabled_desi.

EIGHTEEN
Antisexist Action Plan

If you're not furious about sexism, you haven't been paying attention.

—Lynn Schmidt

If you weren't angry about sexism before reading this book, you should be now. Being angry is a positive emotion, because anger channeled in the right direction leads to change. Unfortunately, women are programmed to believe they are supposed to be kind and nurturing, that it's inappropriate to express anger. Women are taught from an early age that being angry is ugly. Throughout history, angry women have been called crazy, hysterical, psychotic, witches, and bitches. They have been burned at the stake, imprisoned, beaten, drugged, fired from jobs, gaslighted, and cyber-mobbed. Many men and women continue to validate that stereotypical trope.

Women are born with a voice but are discouraged from using it. Society silences women, just as Penelope was silenced in Homer's *Odyssey* 3,000 years ago. There is a likeability penalty that women pay when they are assertive or forceful when angry. Men are allowed to be angry; they are respected for it. Men need to get mad about sexism and step up and join the fight as allies, or better yet, as accomplices.

Women need to get angry about sexism, as their anger will give them the power to change the world. Men and women, you have permission to get mad about the abuse women and girls experience. To get angry about how that abuse shows up as microaggression, discrimination, harassment, and violence.

Why be angry about sexism? Half the world's population, women, are marginalized. Women are experiencing microaggression, discrimination, harassment, and violence in record numbers that continue to grow. The cost of violence and discrimination against women is high, as is the lost opportunity cost to the world's economy. Much of the data indicates that women's rights are not progressing.

In many cases, women's rights have taken steps backward. The gender-equality goals set by the United Nations won't be attained. There isn't one country where women have achieved full equality. The percentage of women in management worldwide is 27 percent, the same rate it has been for twenty-five years. Sexism has a negative impact on women, men, children, and nations.

Being antisexist is the commitment you need to make to help stop sexism. It's up to you to do your part, as almost everyone is sexist to some degree. The majority of men and women commit sexist microaggressions, sometimes unconsciously. These insults are like paper cuts. One paper cut hurts, while many paper cuts leave permanent scars. A smaller subset of men and women practice sexist discrimination. Discrimination causes inequality and lost opportunities for women and girls. Men are responsible for the majority of the harassment and violence that women and girls experience.

Men who use violence against women, who rape and murder women, often build up to it. They begin with microaggression in the form of sexist jokes, insults, and locker-room banter. When that behavior goes unchecked by other men, and women ignore it, the men who use violence against women move on to harassment. They harass women at work, online, or on the street; they use hate speech and expose themselves.

When other men accept the behavior, and they go unprosecuted, these men escalate to using multiple forms of violence to abuse women, including rape and murder. Sometimes that behavior is accepted, and men go unpunished because some believe men should use their power to control women. Men can end sexism. It's time for all men to speak up and take action. Imagine what men could achieve if they worked together to stop sexism.

Women, you are powerful. Don't allow your voices to be silenced. Your opinion matters. Your work matters. Your safety matters. Your life matters. Find the strength and the courage to stand up and speak out. Others will be there to support you. While ending sexism does not rest solely on your shoulders, your help is needed. Women working together can accomplish extraordinary things. Imagine what men and women working together could achieve toward ending sexism.

Four Outcomes of Sexism and the Antisexist Action Plan

The abuse of women needs to stop before microaggression, discrimination, harassment, and violence occur. You can help make that happen by managing your sexism and the sexism of others. The purpose of this book is to present a simple road map for you to use to be antisexist. The three main goals of the book are to:

1. Enable you to understand what sexism is and its impact on women.
2. Help you to manage sexism when you experience it.
3. Assist you in becoming antisexist by challenging sexism, championing women's rights, and creating equality.

Each chapter ends with action planning ideas, including the essays. Go back and review that information. Now is the time to pull all of your ideas together into a plan you can easily follow. For each of the four outcomes of sexism and intersectionality, decide what you want to start doing, stop doing, and continue doing. Becoming antisexist requires unlearning stereotypes and biases about women and girls. It requires calling out sexism when you see it. It requires making changes to systemic sexism in organizations and institutions.

Keep your action plan simple, take the necessary steps to end sexism, and be antisexist. Revisit your plan regularly to see how you are doing, and add new actions as needed. How will you challenge sexism, champion women's rights, and create equality? It's time to stop sexism and create a safe and equitable world for women and girls.

FOUR OUTCOMES OF SEXISM	
Microaggression	**Discrimination**
Sexist Language Stereotypes Objectification Shaming Mansplaining Invalidation	Education Employment Wage Gap Career Healthcare Sexual
Harassment	**Violence**
Verbal Physical Online Bullying Street Flashing	Physical Sexual Emotional Economic Coercive Control Femicide

Microaggression

Start:

Stop:

Continue:

Discrimination

Start:

Stop:

Continue:

Harassment

Start:

Stop:

Continue:

Violence

Start:

Stop:

Continue:

Intersectionality

Start:

Stop:

Continue:

Sexism has never rendered women powerless. It has either suppressed their strength or exploited it.

—BELL HOOKS

Acknowledgements

Writing a book requires many people to work together to deliver the final product. I greatly appreciate the contributions of everyone involved in the creation of *Antisexist*. I received support from friends, family, and professional acquaintances. Thank you to everyone involved.

I want to extend my appreciation to the women and men who contributed personal essays and short stories. Your essays and stories will help readers gain important insights into the impact of sexism. I wish all of you the best as you continue your antisexist journeys. I look forward to continuing these discussions as we all work on challenging sexism, championing women's rights, and creating equality.

Several hundred women completed a survey and took the time to provide me with their perspectives on women's challenges. Thank you for providing your input, which helped shape the book's focus areas.

A special thank you to my book editor Frank Steele and my exterior and interior designer Megan Katsanevakis. Your unique talents enabled the final product to be an impactful and engaging book for the world to read. I learned so much from working with you. I'm looking forward to our next project together.

To my readers, a heartfelt thank you. I appreciate your desire to create a safe and equitable world for women and girls. I wish you success on your journey to be antisexist and manage sexism. Remember, when you see something, say something.

Notes

Chapter 1

Biases: United Nations, UN News, "Report reveals nearly 90 per cent of all people have a deeply ingrained bias against women," March 5, 2020, https://news.un.org/en/story/2020/03/1058731

Women killed daily: UN Women, "Facts and figures: Ending violence against women," last updated January 2022, https://www.unwomen.org/en/what-we-do/ending-violence-against-women/facts-and-figures

Homer: Mary Beard, *Women & Power: A Manifesto,* New York, Liveright Publishing Corporation, 2017

Right to vote: Jody Ellis, "When women got the right to vote in 50 countries," *stacker,* September 21, 2021, https://stacker.com/stories/4299/when-women-got-right-vote-50-countries

1970s: Jessica Hill, "Fact check: Post detailing 9 things women couldn't do before 1971 is mostly right," *USA Today,*

October 28, 2020, https://www.usatoday.com/story/news/
factcheck/2020/10/28/fact-check-9-things-women-couldnt-do-
1971-mostly-right/3677101001/

Six types of sexism: Jayne Leonard, "6 types of sexism, examples,
and their impact," *Medical News Today*, May 27, 2021, https://www.
medicalnewstoday.com/articles/types-of-sexism

Microaggression: Jenee Desmond-Harris, "What exactly is
a microaggression?" *Vox*, February 16, 2015, https://www.vox.
com/2015/2/16/8031073/what-are-microaggressions

Cost of violence: CARE, "Counting the Cost: The Price
Society Pays for Violence Against Women," viewed December
22, 2021, https://www.care-international.org/files/files/
Counting_the_costofViolence

Loss in human capital: The World Bank, "Unrealized Potential:
The High Cost of Gender Inequality in Earnings," May 30, 2018,
www.worldbank.org/en/topic/gender/publication/unrealized-
potential-the-high-cost-of-gender-inequality-in-earnings

Chapter 3

Women and microaggressions: Lean In, Women in the
Workplace 2018, "Everyday discrimination & microaggressions,"
https://leanin.org/women-in-the-workplace-report-2018/
women-get-less-support-less-access-at-work

European microaggressions: Human Rights Channel, "Sexism:
See it. Name it. Stop it.," viewed January 4, 2022, https://human-
rights-channel.coe.int/stop-sexism-en.html

Chapter 6

Global gender gap: World Economic Forum, "Global Gender Gap Report." March 30, 2021, https://www.weforum.org/reports/global-gender-gap-report-2021/digest

Girls education: Azza Karam, United Nations, UN Chronicle, "Education as the Pathway towards Gender Equality," viewed December 12, 2021, https://www.un.org/en/chronicle/article/education-pathway-towards-gender-equality

Unpaid work: UN Women, "Redistribute unpaid work," viewed December 17, 2021, https://www.unwomen.org/en/news/in-focus/csw61/redistribute-unpaid-work

Unpaid care: G. Ferrant, L. Pesando, K. Nowacka, "Unpaid Care Work: The missing link in the analysis of gender gaps in labour outcomes," OECD Development Center, December, 2014, https://www.oecd.org/dev/development-gender/Unpaid_care_work.pdf

Global wage gap: UN Women, "Equal pay for work of equal value," viewed December 4, 2021, https://www.unwomen.org/en/news/in-focus/csw61/equal-pay

US wage gap: R. Bleiweis, J. Frye, R. Khattar, "Women of Color and the Wage Gap," *American Progress*, November 17, 2021, https://www.americanprogress.org/article/women-of-color-and-the-wage-gap/

UK wage gap: Chloe Beevers, "Equal Pay Gap in the UK Widens Again," Morrish Solicitors, LLP, November 16, 2021, https://www.morrishsolicitors.com/equal-pay-gap-in-the-uk-widens-again/

Australia wage gap: Workplace Gender Equality Agency, "Australia's Gender Pay Gap Statistics," August 27, 2021, https://www.wgea.gov.au/publications/australias-gender-pay-gap-statistics

Negotiation: B. Artz, A. Goodall, A. Oswald, "Research: Women Ask for Raises as Often as Men, but Are Less Likely to Get Them," *Harvard Business Review*, June 25, 2018, https://www.wgea.gov.au/publications/australias-gender-pay-gap-statistics

Performance reviews: P. Cecchi-Dimeglio, "How Gender Bias Corrupts Performance Reviews and What to Do About It," *Harvard Business Review*, April 12, 2017,

Performance language: Kieran Snyder, "The abrasiveness trap: High-achieving men and women are described differently in reviews," *Fortune*, August 26, 2014, https://fortune.com/2014/08/26/performance-review-gender-bias/

Promotion rates: Lean In, Women in the Workplace 2021, "The broken rung is still holding women back," https://leanin.org/women-in-the-workplace-2021

Discrimination consequences: Speak Out Revolution, "The Speak Out Dashboard," viewed January 2022, https://www.speakoutrevolution.co.uk/dashboard

Women's healthcare: Renee Goyeneche, "Just Your Imagination? The Dangerous Gender Bias in Women's Healthcare,' *Forbes,* September 21, 2021, https://www.forbes.com/sites/womensmedia/2021/09/21/just-your-imagination-the-dangerous-gender-bias-in-womens-healthcare/?sh=4306c9043e54

Surgery deaths: Denis Campbell, "Women 32% more likely to die after operation by male surgeon study reveals," *The Guardian*, January 4, 2022, https://www.theguardian.com/society/2022/jan/04/women-more-likely-die-operation-male-surgeon-study

Maternal mortality: E. Declercq and L. Zephyrin, "Maternal Mortality in the United States: A Primer," The Commonwealth Fund, December 16, 2020, https://www.commonwealthfund.org/publications/issue-brief-report/2020/dec/maternal-mortality-united-states-primer

Trans women: McKinsey & Company, "Being transgender at work," November 10, 2021, https://www.mckinsey.com/featured-insights/diversity-and-inclusion/being-transgender-at-work

Chapter 9

Sarah Everard: Erica Buist, "Sarah Everard: The missed opportunities to stop Wayne Couzens before he murdered her," *MyLondon*, September 30, 2021, https://www.mylondon.news/news/south-london-news/sarah-everard-missed-opportunities-stop-21720353

Harassment statistics: Rhitu Chatterjee, "A New Survey Finds 81 Percent of Women Have Experienced Sexual Harassment," npr, February 21, 2018, https://www.npr.org/sections/thetwo-way/2018/02/21/587671849/a-new-survey-finds-eighty-percent-of-women-have-experienced-sexual-harassment

Sexual harassment: Speak Out Revolution, "The Speak Out Dashboard," viewed January 2022, https://www.speakoutrevolution. co.uk/dashboard

Online harassment of girls: Plan International, "Abuse and Harassment Driving Girls Off Facebook, Instagram, and Twitter," October 5, 2020, https://plan-international.org/ news/2020-10-05-abuse-and-harassment-driving-girls-facebook-instagram-and-twitter

Online harassment: Nina Jankowicz, "Online Harassment Toward Women is Getting Even More Insidious," *Wired*, January 28, 2021, https://www.wired.com/story/ online-harassment-toward-women-getting-more-insidious/

Bullying: YouthTruth, Bullying 2017, "What do students tell us about bullying?," viewed Janaury 8, 2022, https://youthtruthsurvey. org/bullying-2017/

Street harassment: UN Women, "Prevalence and reporting of sexual harassment in UK public spaces," March 2021, https:// www.unwomenuk.org/site/wp-content/uploads/2021/03/ APPG-UN-Women_Sexual-Harassment-Report_2021

France verbal harassment: Stephanie Fillion, "2 Years Later, What We Can Learn From France's Anti-Catcalling Law," *Forbes*, January 26, 2021, https://www.forbes.com/sites/ stephaniefillion/2021/01/26/2-years-later-what-we-can-learn-from-frances-anti-catcalling-law/

No men for 24 hours: feminist next door, @emrazz, December 24, 2021, "Women, imagine that for 24 hours, there were no men in the world.," Twitter, twitter.com/emrazz?s=11

Flashing: Julie Bindel, "Flashing is a serious sexual offence: treat it as such," *Tortoise*, December 6, 2021, https://www.tortoisemedia.com/2021/12/06/flashing-is-a-serious-sexual-offence-treat-it-as-such/

Indecent exposure: Sirin Kale, "The indecent exposure epidemic: How are they not taking this seriously after Sarah Everard?," *The Guardian*, October 7, 2021, https://www.theguardian.com/world/2021/oct/07/indecent-exposure-flashing-sarah-everard-police-response

Chapter 12

Hannah Clarke: Madonna King, "Intimate terrorism: why the murders of Hannah, Aaliyah, Laianah, and Trey must spark change, " *The Sidney Morning Herald*, November 20, 2020, https://www.smh.com.au/lifestyle/life-and-relationships/intimate-terrorism-why-the-murders-of-hannah-aaliyah-laianah-and-trey-must-spark-change-20200910-p55ubz.html

Three risk factors: Dr. Amanda Gearing, "Criminalisation of Coercive Control in Queensland," June 19, 2021, www.womenstaskforce.qld.gov.au/__data/assets/pdf_file/0005/691214/wsjt-submission-dr-amanda-gearing

Australian detective: BBC News, "Baxter killings: Australian detective stood down for victim blaming," February 21, 2020, https://www.bbc.com/news/world-australia-51583358

Violence against women: UN Women, "Facts and figures: Ending violence against women," last updated January 2022, https://www.unwomen.org/en/what-we-do/ending-violence-against-women/facts-and-figures

EU gender-based violence: European Institute for Gender Equality, "Gender-based violence costs the EU €366 billion a year," July 7, 2021, https://eige.europa.eu/news/gender-based-violence-costs-eu-eu366-billion-year

US cost of domestic violence: B. Lomborg and M. Williams, "The cost of domestic violence is astonishing," *The Washington Post*, February 22, 2018, www.washingtonpost.com/opinions/the-cost-of-domestic-violence-is-astonishing/2018/02/22/f8c9a88a-0cf5-11e8-8b0d-891602206fb7_story.html

Francine Hughes: Emily Langer, "Francine Hughes Wilson, whose burning bed became a TV film, dies at 69," *The Washington Post*, April 1, 2017, https://www.washingtonpost.com/national/francine-hughes-wilson-whose-burning-bed-became-a-tv-film-dies-at-69/2017/03/31/a1799db8-161c-11e7-ada0-1489b735b3a3_story.html

Chanel Miller: Emma Brockes, "Chanel Miller on why she refuses to be reduced to the Brock Turner sexual assault victim," *The Guardian*, September 25, 2019, https://www.theguardian.com/us-news/2019/sep/25/stanford-sexual-assault-victim-chanel-miller-interview

Billie Eilish: Maree Crabbe, "Billie Eilish says 'porn destroyed my brain', the time for being coy has passed," news.com.au, December 18, 2021, https://www-news-com-au.cdn.ampproject.org/c/s/www.news.com.au/lifestyle/relationships/sex/billie-eilish-says-porn-destroyed-my-brain-the-time-for-being-coy-has-passed/news-story/25ccb0a875fe870ac05f55b2c3beeab4?amp

Pornography: Shreya Agrawal, "How exposure to pornography as a child can affect the young mind," *The Indian Express*, January 14, 2022, https://indianexpress.com/article/lifestyle/life-style/children-pornography-porn-dangerous-impacts-early-exposure-violent-graphic-billie-eilish-7709240/

Intimate image abuse: Anna Moore, "I have moments of shame I can't control: the lives ruined by explicit collector culture," *The Guardian*, January 26, 2022, https://amp-theguardian-com.cdn.ampproject.org/c/s/amp.theguardian.com/world/2022/jan/06/i-have-moments-of-shame-i-cant-control-the-lives-ruined-by-explicit-collector-culture

Violence facts: Maria Zafar, "16 shocking facts about violence against women and girls," reliefweb, December 7, 2020, https://reliefweb.int/report/world/16-shocking-facts-about-violence-against-women-and-girls

Sex trafficking: Jasmine Garsd, "Ghislaine Maxwell found guilty of helping Jeffrey Epstein sexually abuse girls," npr, December 29, 2021, https://www.npr.org/2021/12/29/1066219689/ghislaine-maxwell-verdict-trial-jeffrey-epstein

Coercive control: Carol Lambert, "Coercive Control Becoming Criminalized," *Psychology Today*, December 20, 2021, https://www.psychologytoday.com/us/blog/mind-games/202112/coercive-control-becoming-criminalized

Femicide in US: Violence Policy Center, "Nearly 1,800 Women Murdered by Men in One Year, New Violence Policy Center Study Finds," September 29, 2021, https://vpc.org/press/nearly-1800-women-murdered-by-men-in-one-year-new-violence-policy-center-study-finds/

Global Femicide: Douglas Broom, "As the UK publishes its first census of women killed by men, here's a global look at the problem," World Economic Forum, November 25, 2020, https://www.weforum.org/agenda/2020/11/violence-against-women-femicide-census/

Focus on femicide: Jane Gerster, "More men are killed than women, so why focus on violence against women?" *Global News*, February 22, 2020, https://globalnews.ca/news/6536184/gender-based-violence-men-women/

Men stop violence: Mike Cameron, "Dear Men: Partner of murdered Alberta woman challenges men to change," *Edmonton*, October 23, 2018, https://www.cbc.ca/news/canada/edmonton/murder-alberta-1.4871736

Chapter 15

Intersectionality: Merrill Perlman, "The origin of the term intersectionality," *Columbia Journalism Review*, October 23, 2018, https://www.cjr.org/language_corner/intersectionality.php

Sexism and racism: Lean In, Women in the Workplace 2021, "Women of color continue to have a worse experience at work," https://leanin.org/women-in-the-workplace-2021

US wage gap: R. Bleiweis, J. Frye, R. Khattar, "Women of Color and the Wage Gap," *American Progress*, November 17, 2021, https://www.americanprogress.org/article/women-of-color-and-the-wage-gap/

Asian attacks: Marlene Lenthang, "Atlanta shooting and the legacy of misogyny and racism against Asian women," ABC News, March 21, 2021, https://abcnews.go.com/US/ atlanta-shooting-legacy-misogyny-racism-asian-women/ story?id=76533776

Age discrimination: Beth Castle, "Age Discrimination: What It Looks Like & What to Do When It Happens," *INHERSIGHT*, April 16, 2019, https://abcnews.go.com/ US/atlanta-shooting-legacy-misogyny-racism-asian-women/ story?id=76533776

Sexism and ageism: Bonnie Marcus, "Gendered Ageism Affects Women's Job Security and Financial Viability," *Forbes*, September 20, 2021, https://www.forbes.com/sites/bonniemarcus/2021/09/20/ gendered-ageism-affects-womens-job-security-and-financial-viability/

Age discrimination lawsuit: Jennifer Smola, "Two women who won age discrimination settlement sue Ohio State for public records," *The Columbus Dispatch*, July 22, 2019, https://www.dispatch.com/story/news/courts/2019/07/22/ two-women-who-won-age/4628502007/

Sexism and ableism: UN Women, "Women and girls with disabilities," viewed December 19, 2021, https://www.unwomen. org/en/what-we-do/women-and-girls-with-disabilities

Women with disabilities: Human Rights Watch, "Women and Girls with Disabilities," viewed December 10, 2021, https://www. hrw.org/legacy/women/disabled.html

Sexual Abuse: Disability Justice, "Sexual Abuse," viewed December 12, 2021, https://disabilityjustice.org/sexual-abuse/

Allyship: Lean In, Women in the Workplace 2021, "The allyship gap persists," https://leanin.org/women-in-the-workplace-2021

Men as allies: W. B. Johnson and D. G. Smith, "How Men Can Become Better Allies to Women," *Harvard Business Review*, October 12, 2018, https://hbr.org/2018/10/how-men-can-become-better-allies-to-women

About the Author

Dr. Lynn Schmidt is a global talent management consultant with a passion for helping women navigate and avoid career setbacks. She is a certified executive coach specializing in assisting women create careers accompanied by growth and success. Her career focuses on developing leaders in Fortune 500 companies, non-profits, and academia. Lynn was named one of the Women of the Year by the *Idaho Business Review* for her work with women and resilience. She is an advocate for women's rights and gender equality.

Lynn is an award-wining author of six books. Her fifth book, *Thriving from A to Z: Best Practices to Increase Resilience, Satisfaction, and Success* won three literary awards for best personal development book. *Shift Into Thrive: Six Strategies for Women to Unlock the Power of Resiliency*, won six literary awards and is listed in Inc.com as one of the top 60 books about leadership and business written by women. She is a frequent keynote speaker and presenter at conferences worldwide. She presents on a variety of topics including women's rights, gender equality, being antisexist, resiliency, women and career derailment, leadership development, and writing nonfiction books.

Traveling the world is one of Lynn's passions. She also enjoys long walks in nature, photographing the outdoors, hiking foothills trails, going to new restaurants with friends, and spending time with her two shelties.

Get social with Lynn on social media. You can connect with her at Facebook (www.facebook.com/LynnSchmidtAuthor), LinkedIn (https://www.linkedin.com/in/lynnschmidt), Twitter (@LM_Schmidt), and Instagram (@lynnmschmidt). You can learn more at her website schmidtleadership.com and contact her at lschmidt912@hotmail.com.

A Request

Imagine a world without books. Authors need your support to continue to provide the world with the books we all appreciate. If you found this book impactful; found it insightful or helpful, then I'd appreciate it if you would post a short review on Amazon, Barnes & Noble, Bookshop.org, or Goodreads.

Other ways to support authors is to share their posts on social media, tell your family and friends about the book, refer the book to acquaintances, suggest your book club read the book, and ask your library and local bookstore to order the book.

Thank you for your support!
Lynn Schmidt

9 781733 549615